TIMELESS

TIMELESS

Ancient Psalms for the Church Today

Volume One: In the Day of Distress • Psalms 1–41

R. MARK SHIPP
GENERAL EDITOR

Abilene Christian University Press

TIMELESS

Ancient Psalms for the Church Today

ACU PRESS

ISBN 978-0-89112-298-2

Printed in the United States of America

Unless otherwise noted, all Scripture translations are original to this edition.

Associate editors: Cynthia Agnell and Jerry Shipp
Associate music editors: M. L. Daniels and Randy Daw
Associate editor for responsive readings: Jack R. Reese

Title page logo design by Glover Shipp

Cover design by Rick Gibson
Interior text design by Sandy Armstrong

Music Typography by The Paperless Hymnal,® Austin, TX

For information contact:
Abilene Christian University Press
1626 Campus Court
Abilene, Texas 79601

1-877-816-4455
www.abilenechristianuniversitypress.com

11 12 13 14 15 16 / 7 6 5 4 3 2 1

TABLE OF CONTENTS

ACKNOWLEDGMENTS

Several people have been instrumental in bringing volume one of *Timeless* to publication over the past five years. Even before *Timeless* was conceived, Mel Witcher, composer, band director, and educator, was a confidant in discussions about the possibility of such a project. I corresponded in the very beginning with Patrick Miller, professor emeritus of Old Testament at Princeton Theological Seminary, for his wisdom and advice. Some of that correspondence has been incorporated into the Introduction, and my interest in the Psalms and their adoption by the Church are largely due to his instruction and guidance. In the course of the preparation of volume one, Jack Reese, Dean of the Graduate School of Theology at Abilene Christian University, and David Fleer, Professor of Bible and Communication and Special Assistant to the President at Lipscomb University, encouraged me at every stage of the project. Both Jack and David have been valuable "sounding boards" and examples of how one's life and worship should be influenced by the faith and theology of the Psalms.

Several colleagues and co-workers at Austin Graduate School of Theology have provided valuable resources and encouragement. Paramount among these is David Worley, Chancellor of Austin Graduate School of Theology. David's interest in singing the psalms led to the creation of a metrical Psalter evaluation committee, out of which eventually sprang the *Timeless* project. I owe David a debt of gratitude that cannot be repaid. Stan Reid, the President of Austin Graduate School of Theology, has consistently encouraged the project through the many years of its production, as have my faculty colleagues Todd Hall, Allan McNicol, Jeffrey Peterson, and Michael Weed. Of these, Todd and Michael have been particularly helpful with critiques and advice.

Timeless has been blessed with a host of committee members and contributors who believe in the necessity of recovering the Psalms in Christian worship and who have given freely of their time and energies. I cannot mention them all, nor do justice to all those who have sacrificed for this project, but I must mention my editorial assistants, Cynthia Agnell, M. L. Daniels, Randy Daw, and Jerry Shipp. They have labored long hours and their stamp on this project is everywhere and inestimable. It is impossible to overstate the importance of M. L. Daniels, retired chairman of the Music Department at Abilene Christian University, for the production of *Timeless*. Without his involvement, the Psalter portion of this work would not exist. James Tackett, publisher of *The Paperless Hymnal*, has been a committee member and supporter from the beginning. James has provided important musical advice and critiques, did all the musical engraving for this volume, and is the publisher of the paperless version of this project. Libby Weed, principal of Brentwood Christian Elementary School, read the lyrics of all the songs and provided necessary corrections and suggestions, as did Carolyn Thompson, English and German professor at Abilene Christian University. The "*Timeless* Review Committee," comprised of twenty volunteers, including composers, band and orchestra conductors, lyricists, choral conductors, and worship leaders, met every four to six weeks for several years to evaluate music as it was composed. Their names are on the *Timeless Review Committee* page in the introduction to this volume and also appear in the list of contributors at the end of the book. Their work on the volume was vital and their influence is everywhere apparent. I wish to thank in particular three committee members, Randy Daw, Glover Shipp, and Michael Showalter, for carefully proofreading the final proof of this volume and providing helpful corrections.

The Psalter really began several years ago in St. Petersburg, Russia, where I was a guest lecturer at the Institute of Theology and Christian Ministry. As I do not speak Russian, I was cloistered in my apartment every afternoon. Eventually, Konstantin Zhigulin, a student in the Institute, came by with songs he had composed, requesting translation into English. Over the next two weeks we translated about twenty, some of which appear in this volume. I discovered at that time that Konstantin was a brilliant composer of hymns, and also I realized that my half-formulated plans for a new Psalter should begin immediately. This early translation work led to further collaborations and eventually to a hymn composition award at Pepperdine University's *Ascending Voice Symposium II* in 2010 for Psalm 1, "How Blessed Are All Those."

I wish to thank my immediate and extended family for support and involvement in the project. My father, Glover Shipp, bequeathed to us his poet's soul, the results of which can be seen in the numbers of his descendants who have contributed to this volume. He has also contributed several songs, both lyrics and melodies, and continues going strong at the age of 84. My brother, Jerry, has been a songwriting partner of mine for many years and has contributed several lyrics to *Timeless*. My daughters, Sarah and Rachel, have been poets since they were very small, and their contributions to this volume make their dad very proud! Finally, I wish to thank my wife Sheree, who has with patience endured many years of *Timeless* discussions and work. She is indeed the virtuous woman of Proverbs 31.

R. Mark Shipp
Austin Graduate School of Theology
May 8, 2011

Timeless Committee Members

Timeless Review Committee

Cynthia Agnell
Michele Broadway
M. L. Daniels
Randy Daw
Debbie Dorman
Jack Dorman
Katelyn Horn
Norman Horn
Marva Hughes
Bradley H. Merrell
Dan Merrell
Jack Reese
Jerry Shipp
Ruth Ann Somervell
Becky Stewart
James Tackett
Libby Weed
Judy Witcher
Mel Witcher
Melinda Worley

Timeless Lyric Sub-Committee

Cynthia Agnell
Glover Shipp
Jerry Shipp
Mark Shipp
Libby Weed

Timeless Music Sub-Committee

D. J. Bulls
M. L. Daniels
Randy Daw
James Tackett
Mel Witcher

Foreword

The Psalms have a special place in the life of the Christian community, in both our corporate life of worship and our individual lives of faith. On the one hand, they belong to our liturgy and music; on the other hand, they are a guide to prayer and discernment. The Psalms are for study and meditation, and for singing and worship. In the pages that follow, both dimensions of the Psalms are fully manifest. Indeed, they are joined together in a manner that is all too rare. For those who would like to know what the Psalms are about, together and individually, succinct discussions of each psalm provide notes on translation and theological application. Readers will find this a rich resource to illumine the meaning of the Psalms and the way they speak to our life and faith. The writers have made this interpretive work easily accessible, so that whoever picks up a copy of this book may be led immediately into the heart of each psalm, what it says and what it means, how it guides us, and how it gives us words to speak what is on our hearts.

At the same time, readers are presented with the Psalms as they were meant to be from the beginning, a book of hymns, as the Hebrew title of the book tells us. If they are our guide on the pathway of the righteous, as we learn from Psalm 1, they are also from beginning to end the sound of praise to the God who made us and sustains us. Doxology, however, is fully articulated only in music. As one moves through the Psalter, the sound of praise and alleluia, of doxology and glory to God, grows and grows until at the end there is nothing but the music of instruments and voices, orchestras and choruses, everything on earth and in heaven singing and playing to the glory of God. If the Psalms tell us nothing else, they let us, in the words of hymn writer Fred Pratt Green, know that "in our music God is glorified." So it is that after every interpretive presentation of the Psalms in these pages, we move to musical arrangements that turn our thinking into song, our reflection into praise, and our prayers into hymns.

The result is a confirmation and elaboration of the title of this book. For, like all great poetry and music, the Psalms are timeless. Scholars may search for or claim to find the historical context in which a psalm was written, but such efforts are elusive. The Psalms are not tightly tied to their original context. However they have come to us, they are open to the human situation in every time and place.

So take and read, reflect and sing, pray and praise. The Psalms show us the way.

Patrick D. Miller
Louisville, Kentucky
Professor of Old Testament Theology Emeritus
Princeton Theological Seminary
May 30, 2011

Introduction

Why Another Commentary and Metrical Psalter?

I grew up in an environment in Churches of Christ in which few psalms were sung in worship. Indeed, a standard Church of Christ hymnal, *Great Songs of the Church* (Number Two, 1975), holds three sections, including Hymns, Spiritual Songs ("gospel songs"), and Special Songs, but, interestingly, it has no section for Psalms. The "new" *Great Songs* (1986) abandoned any attempt at organization based on song classification (i.e., Col. 3:16) in favor of a modified Trinitarian arrangement—songs of God the Father, Jesus the Son, and songs of the Church and Christian discipleship (presumably songs in some way related to the presence of the Holy Spirit in the Church). When one looks at the scripture index in the back of each volume, one finds that there are 126 references to psalms in the old *Great Songs* and 109 references to psalms in the new *Great Songs*, exclusive of indexed psalm readings. These are by no means all metrical versions (i.e., scripture passages set to Western meter and verse) or paraphrases of psalm texts; most are simply references or allusions to psalm passages. The same remains true with the more recent hymnal, *Songs of Faith and Praise* (1994): there are 199 references to psalms, but only 6 of them are complete psalms, and only 15 reference more than two verses.

I have become increasingly aware of the general Protestant failure to make use of the Psalms in the church's hymnody over the past 100 years and more, although recently there have been some encouraging signs (psalm-singing in the Taizé Community, the forthcoming *Psalms for All Seasons*, Michael Morgan's *The Psalter for Christian Worship*, the *Lutheran Service Book* (Psalm chant section), the *Psalter Hymnal*, and many others). Most Protestant hymnals of the past century have included no more than two or three dozen "psalm hymns," but even these are not really "metrical psalms," but may only quote a few verses or make allusions to a psalm. A comparison of recent hymnals and song collections with those of previous generations demonstrates the paucity of metrical psalm settings in those published more recently. In *The Hymnal for Worship and Celebration* (1986), a popular Evangelical hymnal, there are 105 references or allusions to psalms, but not a single one alluding to or paraphrasing more than two verses. *The Hymnal* (Episcopal Church, 1982) contains metrical versions of 23 psalms out of 720 entries—fairly typical of 20th century hymnals. *The Baptist Hymnal* (1956) has only 11 psalm entries of any kind.

This is a far cry from the practice of Reformed churches of the 16th and 17th centuries, which often sang only psalms in worship! Since that time, there have always been communions that sing the psalms in corporate worship. These include the Christian Reformed Church, the Reformed Presbyterian Church, Eastern Orthodox churches, and many Catholic churches, but by and large, the practice has been marginalized in the age of Contemporary Christian Music.

On the other hand, too often the metrical psalmody of the past forced Hebrew poetry into Western meter and verse. Classic examples of this were metrical Psalters of the 17th and 18th centuries, such as Sternhold's and Hopkins's *Whole Book of Psalms* and the *Whole Booke of Psalmes, Faithfully Translated into English Metre* (the *Bay Psalm Book*). Note this example of less than elegant rendering of Hebrew poetic parallelism into English long meter (8888) in Psalm 100:

> Because Jehovah he is good,
> For ever more is his mercy;
> And unto generations all
> Continue doth his verity.

Too often, the results were not elegant or beautiful, but stilted and forced—at best, awkward English phrasing with sentence structure reversed, strange contractions, and forced rhyme. As Thomas Warton said about the Sternhold and Hopkins Psalter, "[It is] obsolete and contemptible," "an absolute travesty," and "entirely destitute of elegance, spirit, and propriety" (Warton, p. 737).

The tradition of forced metrical psalmody is unnecessary. The metrical psalm need not be verbatim, in the same way that a sermon is not just quoting Scripture, but is one possible exposition of a text, hopefully a faithful one. This is a reason why a composer needs exegetical notes and translations: so that he or she can faithfully represent theological emphases and important terms, and at least have reference to important movements in the structure of the psalm when composing. This most often means looking at "sense units," logical units of thought, more than at verses in the construction of the metrical psalm.

Besides the obvious aesthetic concerns of such metrical Psalters as Sternhold and Hopkins and the *Bay Psalm Book*, there are practical reasons why a "Psalter/Commentary" is needed. First, there is often a disconnect between what happens in the "song service" of many churches and what happens in the sermon, communion, Bible reading, or other parts of worship. Of course, much of this disconnect can be fixed if the quality of the songs selected is high and biblically based. On the other hand (in this disposable, marketing era), worship songs, along with most other music, have a "short shelf life" of weeks or months, and often lack artistic elegance and profound biblical insight. Perhaps the greatest problem with "praise hymns," according to Walter Brueggemann, is the loss of "narrative structure [and] narrative substance," for "when the narrative is lost we are nearly out of business" (personal correspondence, January 13, 2004). Getting a composer (myself included) to consider deeply the text of the Psalms will, we hope, result in better compositions, textually and musically. Second, many churches are unaware of the content and theology of the Psalms. Just to say, "Let's sing the Psalms!" might not get the desired result, because many people wonder why they should sing them. By adding brief, user-friendly notes on the theology, structure, and application for each psalm, we hope to provide one means of bridging that gap.

Finally, while more commentaries and monographs may have been written on the book of Psalms than any other book of the Old Testament, the Psalms were not *primarily* written to be studied, but to be sung and prayed. There is a sense in which the Psalms cannot be completely understood unless and until the modern lamenter uses their vocabulary and movement to once again cry out to the LORD, or the modern worshipper exults in praise with the words and meanings of the hymns. In other words, since the Psalms are lyric poetry, perhaps they cannot be finally comprehended until they are sung. But since this approach is very much *terra incognita* for many individuals and churches, brief comments and notes on each psalm could be particularly helpful for modern worshippers and Bible study teachers.

Substandard poetry and musical settings have not served us well in terms of motivating the church to sing the Psalms. The Church's hymnody is "portable theology" (note Paul's injunction to *teach* one another by means of psalms, hymns and spiritual songs, Col. 3:16) and is, therefore, a major resource for many Christians' understanding of the Christian faith. Furthermore, the book of Psalms is one of the fonts of the vocabulary, theology, and movement of worship in the Bible, the Synagogue, and the Church. Failure to sing and study the Psalms will, over time, impoverish both theology and worship.

All this is to say that 1) not much has been done to promote Psalm singing in recent times; 2) the history of metrical psalmody has largely consisted of awkward poetry and inelegant marriages of texts and tunes; and 3) we can do better.

What Is *Timeless*?

Timeless is a "Psalter/Commentary," combining in-depth study of the Psalms with worship in song. The present volume, encompassing Psalms 1–41 ("book one" of the book of Psalms), is the first of three projected volumes. Volume Two will incorporate books two and three of the book of Psalms (Psalms 42–89). The final volume will incorporate books four and five of the Psalter (Psalms 90–150). The intent of this series is not to produce heavily technical volumes. Rather, they are intended for use by church leaders, ministers, informed lay persons, and Bible teachers to obtain basic understanding of some of the concerns and issues found in a particular psalm, and go from there to worship in song as *an* application of the psalm for the present day.

Timeless has been, from its inception, an ecumenical and international project. While having its origin in the *a cappella* tradition of Churches of Christ, our conviction is that all Christian communions share the original hymnbook of the second temple and the Church. We have, therefore, solicited commentaries, compositions, and lyrics from Methodists, Presbyterians, Baptists, Pentecostals, Roman Catholics, and others.

The entries for each psalm in *Timeless* consist of two sections: the *Commentary* and *Psalter* sections.

The Commentary Section

To provide readers with basic orientation to the content and approach of each psalm, we have included:

1) A new *translation* and, where there are significant variants or difficulties, *translation notes*.
2) *Responsive Readings:* The translations are suitable for public reading. Some of the translations may also be used in public worship settings as responsive readings (i.e., Pss. 1, 2, 3, 4, 5, 6, 7, 8, 11, 15, 19, 20, 22, 23, 24, 25, 27, 30, 32, 34, 38, and 40). They contain, in the left hand margin by the verse numbers, the following signs:

    †: Verses for the leader to read.
    *: Verses for the congregants to read.

3) A *structure and poetry* section, which will locate each psalm within a basic genre (lament, thanksgiving, hymn, "mixed genre," etc.); a basic poetic structure of the psalm, showing its movement and resolution; and perhaps other literary features of the psalm.
4) A *theology and application* section, containing a discussion of the main theological movements and concerns found in the psalm and how the psalm still speaks to the contemporary church.
5) A *synopsis*, or brief recap of the most important theological and practical points derived from the psalm, suitable for public reading. Each of these falls under a heading beginning *For Those Who Sing Psalm #*.

The Psalter Section

Because worship, and especially worship music, is a pressing and often divisive issue, this is the approach we have taken relative to the music:

1) There is a *relationship between truth and beauty*! We try to avoid triteness in every psalm setting and strive for beauty. The Psalms are beautiful—therefore, why not metrical psalmody?
2) Each psalm setting is *based upon the translation, structure, and theology* of the *Commentary* section. In this way, there should be a close connection between the *Commentary* section and this metrical psalm section.

3) There are *two to four musical settings per psalm* (except for Psalm One, which has six): a "traditional" hymn setting and a "contemporary" setting (although the difference between this and the previous can be difficult to define); and sometimes also a verbatim chant or a "special" or "choral" piece. This variety demonstrates several ways of bringing the Psalms into Christian worship. With two or three exceptions, all of these metrical psalms are new compositions for *Timeless*. We are not looking to recover older metrical psalms, but to do something new.
4) The traditional and contemporary settings are *not verbatim repetitions* of the exact words of the psalm (although the chant, by definition, does this). The hymn poetry is based upon each poetic section (the "structure" of the psalm), thereby allowing the lyricist freedom to create words consonant with the flow and structure of the psalm. The metrical psalms, like a sermon, are not exact copies of the text of scripture, but expositions of it.
5) *Companion Stereo Recordings*: Recordings of all the arrangements in *Timeless*, Volume One, are available as they appear here: *Timeless*, Volume 1 Compact Disc (ACU Press).
6) *Electronic Media*: Projectable slides and downloadable pdf files of the music for all the arrangements are available at: www.PaperlessHymnal.com/Timeless.

The "Quill" System

Most of the music in *Timeless* is intended for the average congregation to sing. *Beauty and simplicity is the goal.* Some songs, however, are more challenging and have been included for more musically literate churches and groups. You will notice in the top left hand corner of each song small "writing quills." They designate the degree of difficulty of each song setting:

- One quill indicates a simple setting that requires little or no musical training.
- Two quills indicate a setting slightly more challenging, but one suitable for congregational or devotional purposes.
- Three quills indicate a setting for a church or group with more sophisticated training, but one that may be learned by a motivated congregation.
- Four quills indicate the most challenging setting for congregational singing, but one that may be attempted by churches that are musically literate and highly motivated to learn difficult songs.
- Five quills indicate a setting for choral or special music groups.

Notes on Translation and Poetry

All translations, commentaries, and notes reflect the research and opinions of the respective writers (whose names are found at the end of the "For Those Who Sing Psalm #" sections). All commentators have attempted to follow the guidelines provided to them by the editorial committee. However, commentators in *Timeless*, Volume One, are uniquely responsible for their own comments and conclusions.

In the translations, the divine name (the Lord in most English translations) has been rendered in small capital letters, except for the capital L, in keeping with the RSV and the NRSV translations.

Also in keeping with many modern speech translations, personal pronouns or descriptive terms for God are not capitalized.

Words which are not in the original Hebrew, but are necessary for a smooth English translation, have been designated by italic font style.

Every effort has been made to include technical comments in the translation notes.

Every effort has also been made to use inclusive human language, with the following caveats: 1) for God language, in keeping with most of the nouns, adjectives, and personal pronouns used of God in recent translations, third person, masculine terms have been retained; 2) on occasion, when in hymn lyrics the use of inclusive human language proved too inelegant or difficult, non-inclusive language was allowed for poetic purposes; and 3) non-inclusive human language was allowed in choral settings and chants, again for poetic and aesthetic purposes.

It is our prayer that the Church of Jesus Christ will continue to reclaim the use of the Psalms in Christian worship. It is to this end that the three volumes of *Timeless* are dedicated. May God bless the reading and singing of the "Book of Praises." *Hallelu-yah*!

R. Mark Shipp
Austin Graduate School of Theology
May 8, 2011

Psalm 1

Translation

†1 Blessed is the one who does not walk in the counsel of the wicked, and in the way of sinners does not stand, and in the seat of scoffers does not sit.

*2 Rather, in the instruction[a] of the LORD is his delight, and in his instruction he meditates by day and by night.

†3 And he shall be like a tree planted by streams of water, which produces its fruit in its season; its leaf does not wither, and everything that he does prospers.

*4 The wicked are not so, but are like the chaff which wind drives away.

*5 Therefore the wicked will not stand in the judgment, or sinners in the congregation of the righteous,

*6 for the LORD knows the way of the righteous, but the way of the wicked will perish.

[a] *Torah* is teaching or instruction. It includes law, but also narrative, ritual, and sermon. It has traditionally been translated "law" because of the Greek Septuagint version's *nomos*, "law."

Structure and Poetry

Psalm 1 is the first of two introductions to the book of Psalms, the "Psalter." Serving as an introduction to the entire collection of psalms, it has no title or attribution. It introduces the psalms as wisdom writings—the wise person is the one who prays, meditates, and sings the full counsel of wisdom (lament, thanksgiving, and praise) to be found in the book of Psalms.

Besides being a Wisdom Psalm, Psalm 1 is also a Torah Psalm, connecting meditation on Torah with righteousness. Torah is not only a primary theme in this psalm. Its placement at the beginning of the collection suggests that all 150 psalms should be understood as Torah, God's righteous instruction. This connection of the Psalter with Torah is underscored by its organization into five books, like the Pentateuch: Psalms 1–41 (book 1), 42–72 (book 2), 73–89 (book 3), 90–106 (book 4), and 107–150 (book 5). Also significant for the structure of the Psalter are the three "Torah Psalms": Psalms 1, 19, and 119. The ordering of these particular psalms cannot be accidental: in the same way that Torah provides order and structure for the life disciplined by it, the Torah Psalms demonstrate the same order and perfection in their placement in the Psalter.

The division of Psalm 1 into three sections accentuates the value of Torah for wise and righteous living. First, verses 1–3 describe the *way of the righteous.* Verse 1 describes what they are not like—they do not commune with the wicked in any fashion (elaborated in three postures, walking, standing, and sitting). Verse 2 describes what they do (meditate on Torah) and what they are like (a healthy tree, receiving sustenance, deeply rooted, and producing fruit).

Second, verses 4–5 describe the *way of the wicked*. Verse 4 states what they are *not* like: not like the righteous in verses 1–3. Verse 5 states what they *are* like (dead plant matter, with no sustenance or roots) and what they will *not* do (stand with the righteous).

Verse 6 is the *conclusion* to this brief Torah/Wisdom Psalm concerning the righteous and the wicked. Two *ways* have been set forth in the psalm: the way of the righteous, also the way of wisdom and meditation on Torah, and the way of the wicked, that of folly. The righteous way is known by God (suggesting intimate, covenant knowledge), while the way of folly/wickedness will not survive.

Theology and Application

Several wisdom terms are used in this psalm. Foremost among these is Torah, instruction. In the book of the Torah, the books of Moses or the Pentateuch, instruction occurs as story and as the "walk," or manner of life dependent upon that story. There are only two ways within which one can walk, according to verses 1 and 6: the righteous way, which is characterized by meditation upon Torah and is deeply rooted, stable, and productive, and the wicked way, which is not characterized by Torah and is the opposite of the fertile, productive, and stable tree (v. 3). The wicked way is ephemeral and lacking in substance—dead plant matter, with no life, nourishment, or productivity.

As with ancient Israel, meditating upon God's teaching (Scripture, the history of God's mighty works, the tradition of the prophets and apostles) is *wise*. It also enables one to have deep roots in life, with health and fruitfulness. To be wicked is to fail to do these things. To be foolish is to not meditate on Torah and results in no stability, fruitfulness, or substance. What is the part of God in all this? He *knows* the way of righteous people. He recognizes and supports the one who seeks his way with the whole heart. The way of the wicked, on the other hand, is completely opposite. God does not recognize (maintain covenant commitment with) those who are foolish.

For Those Who Sing Psalm 1

Psalm 1 compares the two ways: the way of the righteous and the way of the wicked. Verses 1–3 compare the righteous person to a stately tree, productive of fruit, deeply rooted, and full of life and vitality. The righteous one does not walk in the way of the wicked; that is, one whose manner of life is distinct from those who walk in evil. The walk of the righteous is in the "way of Torah" (God's instruction). Verses 4–5 compare this way with the way of the wicked. The way of the wicked is simply "not so": there is no life, no rootedness, no vitality, but they are like dead plant matter. Verse 6 concludes with a brief comparison of the two ways: the righteous way is commended by God, but the wicked way leads to death.

Psalm 1 is a beautiful and fitting introduction to the book of Psalms as a whole. It suggests that the entire collection of psalms deals with God's righteous instruction and the wisdom to be gained by meditating upon it and walking in its way.

Mark Shipp

How Blessed

Psalm 1

Mark Shipp & Randy Daw

Ruth Ann Somervell & Debbie Dorman

God's Favor

Psalm 1

Mel Witcher

Mel Witcher

How Blessed Are All Those

Psalm 1

Mark Shipp

Konstantin Zhigulin

do they stand in sin - ners' paths, nor do they sit with them; but
yield their fruit in seas - on and in right-eous-ness a - bound. The
con - gre - ga - tions of the just, nor walk with - in their way; for
law they med - i -
far a - way and
walk in wick - ed -
in the right - eous law of God is their de - light, and
wick - ed are not so, but they are like the chaff that
God knows right - eous ones, who trust him from their birth, but
tate by day and
none shall speak on
ness will per - ish
1, 2
on this law they med - i - tate by day and then
wind drives far a - way and none shall speak on their
all who walk in wick - ed - ness will
then by night.
their be - half.
from the
3
rit.
per - ish from the earth! who do not walk in sin.
earth! How bless-ed are all those who do not walk in sin.

Choral
Mark Shipp

How Blest Is the Man

Psalm 1

Mark Shipp
Arr. M. L. Daniels

How Blest Is the Man

Blessed Is the Man Who Trusts in God

Psalm 1

Choral
Mark Shipp

Konstantin Zhigulin

Blessed Is the Man Who Trusts in God

Psalm One

Chant
Translation by Mark Shipp

A. H. D. Troyte (Troyte's chant #1)
Voicing by Mel Witcher

Psalm 2

Translation

†1 Why are the nations in a tumult, and the peoples plan vainly?
*2 The kings of the earth stationed themselves, and the rulers took counsel together against the Lord and against his Messiah:
*3 "Let us tear off his bonds, and let us cast his cords from us."

†4 The one who sits in heaven laughs; the Lord mocks them.
†5 Then he will speak to them in his anger, and in his wrath he will terrify them:
*6 "I have installed my king on Zion, my holy hill."

†7 I will tell the statute of the Lord: he said to me, "You are my son, today I have begotten you.
*8 Ask of me and I will give the nations *as* your inheritance and the ends of the earth your possession.
*9 You will break them with a scepter of iron, you will shatter them like a potter's vessel."

†10 And now, O kings, be wise; be warned, O judges of the earth.
*11 Serve the Lord with fear, and writhe with trembling;
*12 Kiss the son, lest he be angry and you perish *in the way*, for his anger is kindled quickly. Blessed are all who take refuge in him.

Structure and Poetry

Psalm 2 is the second introduction to the Psalter. As with Psalm 1, it has no superscription or title. Psalm 2 is a Royal, or Messianic Psalm, that is, a psalm dealing with God's choice of David and his descendants as kings in Jerusalem. Psalm 2 is the invitation to read the Psalms messianically, as the book that has its most complete application in the life, ministry, and death of Jesus, the son of David.

The Royal Psalms help provide structure to the book of Psalms as a whole. Books 1 and 2 of the Psalter (Pss. 1–72) are mostly "Psalms of David," beginning (Ps. 2) and ending (Ps. 72) with Royal Psalms of Davidic kingship. Book 3 likewise ends with a Royal Psalm (Ps. 89), this one lamenting the demise of kingship and exile to Babylon. Instead of Royal Psalms, book 4 (Pss. 90–106) is characterized by Enthronement Psalms of God's kingship, reflecting the idea that, though human kingship may fail, God remains sovereign over the nations. Jesus, the true son of David, combines the emphases of both the

Royal Psalms of David's royal line (Matt 1:1) and the Enthronement Psalms (God is the true king over Israel and the world).

The structure of the psalm is simple: a change of speaker signals a change of section, with four sections to the poem:

Verses 1–3:	The nations plot against the king in Jerusalem.
Verses 4–6:	The LORD laughs at their conspiracies, because of his anointed Messiah on Zion.
Verses 7–9:	The LORD grants sonship, a scepter, and victory to the king (the speaker).
Verses 10–12:	The warning of the king to the nations to serve him and the LORD or suffer the consequences.

Theology and Application

This psalm illustrates God's election of David and his descendants as kings and his election of Zion (the temple mount and, by extension, the city of Jerusalem) as the site of the temple, where his "name" was enthroned. The thought world of this psalm is very different from ours. It presumes kingship and dominion of the anointed king over other nations. God has selected his anointed one, the son of David, to reign and exercise dominion. It is in vain that the nations conspire, for God has chosen the son of David and granted him sonship. Indeed, he has given the king dominion over those very nations. So, they must be wise and not revolt, for God will not take kindly to this. Psalm 2 illustrates the "Zion theology," based on the covenant with David in 2 Samuel 7: God's eternal choice of David and Zion. The chaos or tumult of the nations is found in many other similar passages (see Pss. 46 and 48): they may come against Jerusalem, but God will not allow them to succeed, for Jerusalem is his dwelling place and the throne of the son of David.

"Today I have begotten you" is probably the language of coronation. When the Davidic king took the throne, he became "God's son," with a very special relationship and closeness to God as his "father."

Royal Psalms are among the hardest for us to apply, as their world seems so different from ours. On the other hand, they invite us to read the psalms messianically, or, as Dietrich Bonhoeffer puts it, to read the Psalms as the book of Christ. If we read this psalm as strictly relating to an old system of government and a historical setting long gone, it is indeed difficult to find the relevance for ourselves. But if we see that the psalm relates to any son of David, installed as king and holding dominion over all the nations of the earth, then Jesus the Messiah fulfills this role as the truly anointed son of David, the divine son of the heavenly king. The nations would still do well to accept his warning and rebuke.

For Those Who Sing Psalm 2

In Psalm 2, God has chosen his anointed one, the son of David, to reign and exercise dominion over the nations of the earth. It is in vain that these nations conspire, for God has chosen the descendants of David and granted them sonship. When Israel's king took the throne, he became God's son with a very special relationship to God as his father. Jesus fulfills this role as the true and ideal son of David, the anointed king and divine son of the heavenly king. The nations would still do well to heed his warning and rebuke.

Psalm 2 is the second introduction to the book of Psalms. It invites us to read the Psalms messianically, as the prayers of Jesus, the anointed son of David, who still rules over the nations.

Mark Shipp

Why Do the Nations Rage?

Psalm 2

Mark Shipp | Mark Shipp & Randy Daw

He Has Set His King in Zion

Psalm 2

Marva L. Hughes — Marva L. Hughes

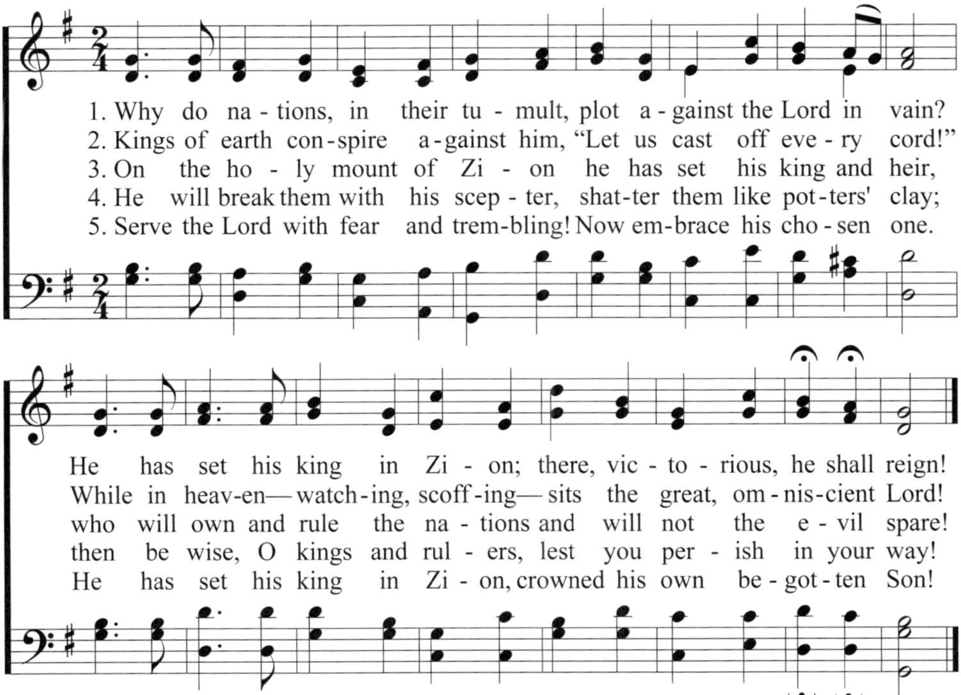

Why Are the Nations in a Tumult?

Psalm 2

Translation by Mark Shipp

Chant setting by Mel Witcher

Psalm 3

Translation

A song of[a] David, when he fled from Absalom his son.[b]

†1 O Lord, how my adversaries have become many; many are arising against me.
†2 Many are saying to my soul, "There is no salvation for him with God!" [*Selah*][c]

*3 But you, O Lord, are a shield about me, my glory and the lifter of my head.
†4 I cry out my voice to the Lord, and he answers me from his holy mountain [*Selah*].
*5 I lie down and I sleep; I awaken, for the Lord sustains me.
†6 I will not fear ten thousands of people who have set *themselves* round about against me.

*7 Arise, O Lord; save me, my God, for you have smitten all my enemies *on the* cheek,
you have broken the teeth of the wicked.

*8 Salvation *belongs* to the Lord. Upon your people be your blessing.

[a] In Hebrew, *le-dawîd* may imply authorship, ownership, the editor or compiler, and a host of other possibilities.

[b] Beginning with Psalm 3 and continuing throughout most of the Psalter, the superscription is verse 1 in the Hebrew. In the English, the superscription is not assigned a verse number. This results in a one verse difference between most psalms in the Hebrew and their English translations.

[c] *Selah* is an obscure term found in several of the psalms. It may be some kind of performance instruction, such as "pause."

Structure and Poetry

Is this a trust psalm or a lament? This distinction affects the psalm's structure.

The *lament* is a structured cry to the Lord. It generally has two main sections: a lament section and a response or resolution section. All laments contain at least a complaint and a petition, and most have some sort of resolution, including a statement that God has heard the psalmist's cry, vows, and calls to praise. Trust psalms, such as Psalm 23, may have some of the same elements as the lament, but the focus is on God's provision and presence, rather than on the cry for help.

As a lament

Verses 1–2:	The nature of the complaint (enemies).
Verses 3–6:	Trust assertions.
Verse 7:	Petition (save me).
Verse 8:	Response: trust assertion and final blessing.

As a trust psalm

Verses 1–2:	The nature of the complaint—the enemies.
Verses 3–4:	Trust that God saves from the enemies.
Verses 5–6:	Trust in the LORD's sustaining and protecting power.
Verse 7:	Petition for the LORD to continue to deliver, because of God's deliverance in the past.
Verse 8:	Trust assertion/praise and final blessing.

Theology and Application

Psalm 3 is the first lament in the book of Psalms. Laments make up almost half of the Psalter. They are structured cries to the LORD. This particular psalm is difficult to classify, but has some characteristics of the lament and some of the trust psalm.

Laments virtually always have a section that includes a complaint or lament, memory of the past goodness or deliverance of the LORD, and a petition. Generally, there is an abrupt switch to praise after the complaint section—the response section—which might include trust statements, vows, calls to praise, wisdom statements, or a doxology. If this is a lament, it has a very brief response section (v. 8), including a praise or trust statement and a final blessing or benediction. In this psalm, the nature of the complaint involves the enemy. The nature of the enemy is not generally specified in the Psalter. In this case, the enemy appears to be a military foe, that is, a literal enemy.

The psalm is also a trust psalm. Because the psalmist realizes the nature of the LORD is to answer all those who cry out to him, he can rely on the LORD now, even if thousands of the enemy have him surrounded.

On the other hand, the psalmist also makes his petition, in spite of his trust in the LORD. To cry out for deliverance was not simply a thing of the past—there continues to be a need for the psalmist to cry out to the LORD in the present.

For the Christian, the lament is not somehow the absence of faith, or denial of the active presence of the LORD in the life of the believer. It is not just that the psalmist cries out—all people do so in adverse circumstances. It is that the psalmist cries out to the LORD, demonstrating faith at the margins of human experience, when the "chips are down." We are not only, however, the people who voice our laments to the LORD; as with this psalm, our cries are interspersed with the conviction and trust that God will respond to all who cry out to him.

For Those Who Sing Psalm 3

This psalm is a lament, a cry to the LORD for help. The psalmist cries out to the LORD for relief from the persecution of enemies. It is also a psalm of trust. The psalmist realizes that the commitment of the LORD is to respond to all those who cry out to him, so he can rely on the LORD in complete trust in spite of the number and strength of the enemy. To fail to cry out indicates a lack of faith. To voice the complaint and ask God for intervention is an expression of faith.

Mark Shipp

You, O Lord, Are a Shield

Psalm 3

Mark Shipp

Mark Shipp
Arr. M. L. Daniels

You, O Lord, Are a Shield

Strong Defender

Psalm 3

Debbie Dorman

Debbie Dorman
Arr. James W. Tackett

Strong Defender

Psalm 4

Translation

For the choir master.*[a] *With stringed instruments.*[b] *A song of David.

*1 Answer me when I call, O my righteous God! In distress, you made room for me. Be gracious to me and hear my prayer.

†2 O sons of men, how long *will* my glory be shame? Will you love vanity *and* seek falsehood? [*Selah*]

*3 And know that the LORD separates the faithful for himself; the LORD hears when I call to him.

†4 Be angry and do not sin; speak in your hearts upon your bed and be silent [*Selah*].

†5 Sacrifice righteous sacrifices and trust in the LORD.

*6 Many are saying, "Who will make us see good?" Lift upon us the light of your face, O LORD.

*7 You put more joy in my heart than when their grain and their wine abound.

*8 In peace I will both lie down and sleep, for you alone, O LORD, make me dwell securely.

[a] Translation of the Hebrew *lamnasseah*, an obscure term that may have to do with musical direction.

[b] The term *negînah* is an obscure term, but may refer to either a mode of singing (i.e., on a stringed instrument) or a type of song. There are several occurrences of this term in the Psalter, suggesting its technical, musical nature (see the superscriptions of Pss. 6, 54, 55, 67, 76, and Hab. 3:19).

Structure and Poetry

Like the previous psalm, this one has some of the elements of the trust psalm and some of the lament.

Verses 1–2:	Introduction (petition, contrast motif).
Verses 3–5:	Exhortation to the faithful, who are ready to give up.
Verse 6:	Nature of the complaint ("we are doomed"), and petition.
Verses 7–8:	Response section: statement of God's goodness/trust.

Theology and Application

This one is very different from the previous psalm, in that it seems to involve a group. God is reliable, because he answers when people cry out. The psalmist cries out and expects God to answer again.

The psalmist is exhorting the community to faithfulness (*hesed*, "steadfast love"), prayer, indignation ("be angry"), and sacrifice. These he calls "trust." The problem is that the community does not seem to be able to see the LORD's help or intervention ("Who will make us see the good?"). The psalmist cries to the LORD on behalf of the community ("Lift up the light of your face, O LORD"), and the psalmist celebrates the LORD's response (vv. 7–8).

One of the most consistent promises in Scripture is that the LORD hears and responds to those who cry out to him. We often do not receive from God's hand because we do not ask (see Matt. 7:7–12), or we ask from improper motives (James 4:3). This psalm exhorts us to trust and to continue our communion with the LORD in prayer and worship, especially when times are difficult. God knows those who are faithful and hears when they pray to him.

For Those Who Sing Psalm 4

This psalm is a lament of the individual, but also seems to involve a community of faith. God is reliable. Because he answers the psalmist's cries, he can be expected to answer the community's cries as well. The psalmist exhorts the community to faithfulness, prayer, and sacrifice. These things the psalmist calls "trust." However, the community has difficulty seeing the LORD's help or intervention. Therefore the psalmist cries to the LORD on behalf of the community ("Lift up the light of your face, O LORD"), and the psalmist celebrates the LORD's response (vv. 7–8).

Mark Shipp

Answer Me

Psalm 4

Debbie Dorman

Debbie Dorman
Arr. James W. Tackett

rest and safe - ty my God pro - vides; noth - ing com - pares.
rest and safe - ty our God pro - vides; noth - ing com - pares.
last time only
Al - le - lu - ia, al - le - lu - ia, al - le - lu - ia.
A - men, a - men, a - men.

Answer Me When I Call

Psalm 4

Mark Shipp

Mark Shipp
Arr. Konstantin Zhigulin

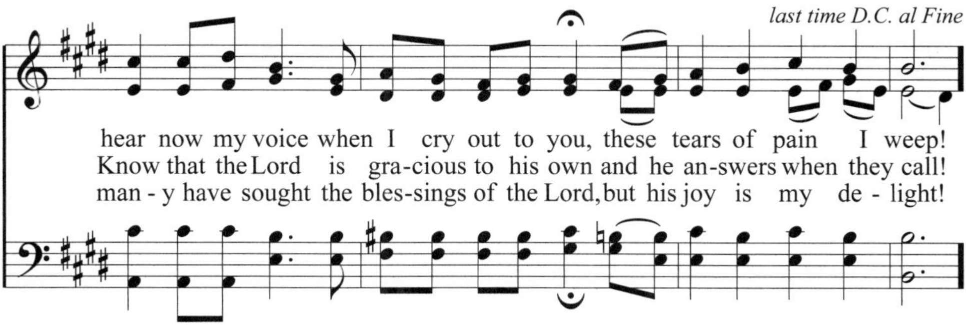
last time D.C. al Fine
hear now my voice when I cry out to you, these tears of pain I weep!
Know that the Lord is gra-cious to his own and he an-swers when they call!
man - y have sought the bles-sings of the Lord, but his joy is my de - light!

Psalm 5

Translation

For the choir master. For the Nehiloth.[a] A song of David.

†1 Give ear to my words, O Lord; consider my groaning.
†2 Listen to the sound of my cry, my king and my God, for unto you I pray!
*3 O Lord, *in the* morning you will hear my voice; I will prepare my argument[b] to you and watch.

*4 You are not a God *who* delights in wickedness; evil will not abide *with* you.
†5 The boastful will not stand before your eyes; you hate all who work iniquity.
†6 You destroy those who speak lies; the man of blood and deceit the Lord detests.

*7 But I, in the abundance of your steadfast loyalty,[c] will come to your house; I will worship toward your holy temple in your reverence.[d]

*8 O Lord, lead me in your righteousness on account of my enemies; make straight your paths before me.
†9 For there is nothing right in their mouth; within them is destruction. Their throat is an open grave; they flatter *with* their tongue.
†10 Declare them guilty, O God; let their counsels fall *and* banish them because of the abundance of their transgressions, for they have rebelled against you.

*11 But let all who take refuge in you rejoice forever; let them sing for joy. Overshadow them, and let those who love your name exult in you.
*12 For you bless the righteous, O Lord; like a shield[e] you surround them *with* favor.

[a] RSV says "for the flutes." The Greek Septuagint says "For the inheritors."

[b] RSV says "in the morning I prepare a sacrifice for thee, and watch." The Hebrew says "I set in order [a sacrifice?]." The Hebrew *`araq* may mean to arrange a sacrifice, but it also means to "lay out an argument." Considering that the verse is about speech, the latter is much more likely.

[c] *hesed* is most often translated "steadfast love" or "lovingkindness." The root meaning of the word is more probably "loyalty," or "loving loyalty."

[d] Literally "fear." Fear has the connotation in Hebrew of reverence, awe and worship, not only terror.

[e] The Greek says "for you bless the righteous like armor; you crown us with favor." The question is whether "shield" goes with "bless" or "crown/surround." It could go either way.

Structure and Poetry

This psalm may be either a trust psalm or a lament. It is possible that it is a trust psalm, like Psalm 23, because there is not a clear response section. On the other hand, the psalm unequivocally begins with words of lament. It probably is, therefore, a lament, with the following structure:

Verses 1–3 (introduction):	This introduction is also a general petition for God to hear the words, the prayer, and the groaning of the psalmist.
Verses 4–10 (*complaint*):	This is unusual, because it is full of general wisdom statements of God's nature. It can be subdivided as follows:
Verses 4–6 (*wisdom statements*):	God hears the righteous, but the boastful, deceitful, and liars he detests.
Verse 7 (*vows*):	The psalmist's vows to praise and worship.
Verses 8–10 (*specific petitions*):	The psalmist prays for God to make straight paths for him, because his enemies have twisted paths. Therefore, he prays that they may they be found guilty, because of their sinful counsels and transgressions.
Verses 11–12 (*response*):	Possibly, verse 11 is yet another petition to protect the righteous, while verse 12 is a statement of God's reliability for those who fear him.

Verses 11–12 may be a response section, because they do not use imperatives, as verses 8 and 10 do ("lead!" "Declare them guilty!"), but rather third person commands ("jussives"): "Let them rejoice, let them sing, let them exult." It is a final call for the righteous to praise, in the form of a petition.

Theology and Application

This psalm is about speech, as can be seen in the introductory petitions ("hear," "consider," "my words," "groaning," "arguments"). The enemies in the lament section are guilty of lies, deceit, flattery, false counsels, and boasting.

The wicked (those who practice such things) cannot "abide" or "sojourn" with God (vv. 4–6); the psalmist, on the other hand, confident in the LORD's covenant loyalty, will enter into the temple and worship (v. 7). His petition is that he may have "straight paths," because his enemies' paths are convoluted and their speech corrupt. His second petition is that those evil people bear the guilt of their evil counsels (v. 10).

If this is a lament and not a trust psalm, verses 11–12 are general petitions for those who love God and who seek refuge in him to rejoice, for they find their protection and blessing in him (v. 12).

In Psalm 5, the psalmist prepares his words as a kind of "court brief" to God, the righteous judge. He prepares his argument carefully, holding nothing back. The psalmist is confident that he may come into the LORD's presence in worship, for he reveres the LORD, trusts in his loyalty, and appeals to his righteousness. The wicked, on the other hand, are guilty of flattery, deceit, and false counsel. The case of the wicked, which has perhaps been taken up against the psalmist with false accusation, will not be accepted by the divine judge, but they will be declared guilty.

There is a warning and a comfort implicit in this psalm. The warning can be for us, if we misuse words, misrepresent others' character or actions, and bring false accusation against them. The comfort is for all who suffer under such evil speech, that God may still be relied upon to hear our cries, judge rightly and compassionately, and protect all who seek refuge in him.

For Those Who Sing Psalm 5

Psalm 5 is about speech. It is the sad truth that we sometimes suffer not for our own evil words, but because of others' false accusations or evil counsel. The words of those who may wish us ill can be extremely damaging. If their words are lies, but they are influential, the results of such false judgment against us can be devastating. We may, on the other hand, do what the psalmist does when confronted with evil counsels and falsehood: he turns to the LORD as the true and righteous judge and requests vindication. God is the only judge who can always be relied upon to be just in judgment, but compassionate to those who cry out to him.

Mark Shipp

Hear My Cry, O Lord

Psalm 5

Marva L. Hughes

Marva L. Hughes

Give Ear unto My Words

Psalm 5

Mark Shipp

Mark Shipp
Arr. M. L. Daniels

Psalm 6

Translation

For the leader[a] with stringed instruments. A song of David.

*[1] O LORD, do not judge me in your anger and do not discipline me in your displeasure.

*[2] Be gracious to me LORD, for I am wasting away; heal me LORD, for I am fearful to the bone.

†[3] My soul is greatly anxious; yet you, LORD! How long?

†[4] Turn, LORD, and save me; deliver me on account of your steadfast love.

†[5] For in death there is no remembrance of you; when gone, who will praise you?

†[6] I am worn out from my groaning; every night I flood my bed, I drench it with my tears.

†[7] My eyes have gone bad from this vexation; they are weak from all my troubles.

*[8] Back off, evildoers; the LORD has heard my crying.

*[9] The LORD has heard my plea; he accepts my prayer.

*[10] All my enemies will be shamed and greatly fearful; they shall turn about and be shamed in a moment.

[a] This is the same Hebrew word translated "choir master" (Pss. 3–5) and "director" (Ps. 39), found often in the Psalms.

Structure and Poetry

This psalm has the classic form of a lament, giving voice to personal troubles and their effects upon the one who prays, especially in relationship with the LORD. Verses 1–5 are a plea to God from one whose self-description has elements of physical and emotional pain. Verses 6–7 elaborate on the author's oppressive circumstances. Verses 8–9 affirm that the LORD has heard and accepted the plea for forgiveness and restoration. Verse 10 is an affirmation that the enemies (the evildoers of v. 8) will be put to shame. They who have caused sickness and fear will themselves be fearful and shamed. This will be the work of the LORD's justice.

The poetry has reinforcing lines that give shape to the psalm by repeating key themes. Repetition of words also reinforces those themes. For example, verses 2 and 3 use the verb "be terrified, fearful, agitated" (*bahal*) to describe the state of the one who prays. Verse 10 uses it to describe those who have afflicted and oppressed the one who prays. In vindicating the one who seeks his forgiveness, the LORD "turns the tables" on the oppressors.

Theology and Application

The psalm is predicated on the belief that the demise of the one who prays would mean the end of communion with God. That is the function of verse 5. The psalmist's horizon does not extend past *Sheol* (the place of the departed) and its separation from the living God. In raising Jesus from the dead, God has demonstrated his power even over the forces and circumstances of death. This offers added comfort from the perspective of Christian faith.

The author fears shame and dying, and so cries out to the LORD for improvement of his circumstances. The psalm is at the same time a plea for a gracious reception by God and forgiveness for any wrongs that the author may have committed. Deliverance comes from the LORD's steadfastness (*hesed*).

In the Catholic (or ancient Western) Church, Psalm 6 is considered a Penitential Psalm. The psalm is one illustration of the classic line, "Take it to the LORD in prayer." It also recognizes the link between "healing" (broadly understood), shamed circumstances, and forgiveness.

For Those Who Sing Psalm 6

God is a God of salvation. There are circumstances in life in which our need is apparent and matters press against us. We can and should turn to the one who has our lives in his hands. Evil is real and oppressive, and God can be trusted to deal with it, including death itself. Oppressive circumstances weigh against us over time. We are invited to offer our fears and terror to the LORD, along with our praise for his constancy and goodness.

Andrew Dearman

Return, O Lord

Psalm 6

Mark Shipp

Konstantin Zhigulin

grave?
prayer.
Re-turn, O Lord, res-cue my soul;
you from the grave? O Lord, res-cue my soul;
my hum-ble prayer. Re-turn, O Lord, res-cue my
grave? O Lord, res-cue my soul;
prayer.
save me be-cause of your lov-ing-kind-ness. Re-turn, O Lord,
save me O God. O Lord,
soul, O God. Re-turn, O Lord,
save me O God. O Lord,
res-cue my soul; save me be-cause of your love.
res-cue my soul; save me be-cause of your love.
res-cue my soul be-cause of your love.
res-cue my soul; save me be-cause of your love.

Lamentation in the Night

Psalm 6

Mark Shipp

Mark Shipp
Arr. Ruth Ann Somervell

Lamentation in the Night

Psalm 7

Translation

A shiggaion[a] of David, which he sang to the Lord concerning Cush, a Benjaminite.[b]

*1 O Lord, my God, in you I take refuge; save me from all my pursuers, and deliver me,
*2 or like a lion they will tear me apart; snatch away, with no one to rescue.

†3 O Lord, my God, if I have done this, if there is wrong in my hands,
†4 if I have treated a friend badly or acted without cause against a foe,
†5 then let the enemy chase and catch me, smash me to the ground, and leave me in the dust. [*Selah*]

*6 Rise up, O Lord, in your anger. Stand up against the fury of my enemies. Wake up, O my God; you have declared judgment.
*7 Let the assembly of the peoples be gathered around you, and over it take your seat[c] on high.

†8 The Lord judges the peoples; judge me, O Lord, according to my righteousness and according to the integrity that is in me.
*9 Let the evil of the wicked come to an end, but support the righteous, you who test the hearts and minds, O righteous God.

†10 God is my shield,[d] he who saves the upright in heart.
†11 God is a righteous judge, and a God who is indignant *about injustice* every day.
*12 If one does not repent, God prepares his sword; he is ready to shoot his bow.
*13 He has prepared his deadly weapons, making his arrows fiery shafts.
†14 See how they conceive evil, and are pregnant with mischief, and give birth to lies!
†15 They make a pit, digging it out, and fall into the hole that they have made.
†16 Their mischief comes back on them, and their violence falls on top of them.

*17 I will give to the Lord the thanks due to his righteousness and sing praise to the name of the Lord, the Most High.

[a] The etymology and meaning of *shiggaion* are uncertain, but the term may mean a lamentation or an ecstatic verse. It also occurs in a slightly different form in Hab. 3:1.

[b] This historical reference is not otherwise corroborated in Scripture. It may relate to a false accusation against David by a certain Benjaminite, of the tribe of Saul.

[c] This translation presupposes a slight change from the Hebrew, which has the verb "return" rather than "sit." In Hebrew, the words are similar.

[d] The Hebrew text has a preposition "upon" that is either superfluous or a portion of a longer term.

Structure and Poetry

In distinction from Psalm 6, where penitence is a part of the psalmist's approach to God, Psalm 7 has affirmations of innocence (vv. 3–5, 8) and pleas to God for vindication (vv. 1–2, 6–7, 9). These two things are the core issues of Psalm 7. Verses 10–16, then, affirm the righteousness of God and his judgment to be worked out against the wicked. The final verse functions like a vow and declares God worthy of praise.

As is common to laments of this type, the work of wicked people and the insidious power of evil are given description (vv. 2, 14) as these elements affect the one who prays. There is a sense in which the evil depicted has its own built-in "self-destruct" mechanism (vv. 15–16), or perhaps its failure is self-incurred.

Theology and Application

There are three "actors" in the drama reflected in the psalm: God, the psalmist, and those who do evil, who afflict the psalmist and oppose the will and purpose of God. God is a righteous judge, indignant at evil, and a shield to those whom he loves and protects. His righteousness is depicted as overseeing the process of evil's demise and in vindicating the one who seeks his protection. God's righteousness is his integrity in action.

The psalmist asserts his innocence. This does not mean a false sense of general rectitude or inappropriate self-confidence. It indicates that in this specific struggle with the power of evil and the specifics of his situation, the psalmist is innocent of wrongdoing. Evildoers ultimately will be frustrated in their designs and thwarted. Note Psalm 1:6: "God knows the way of the righteous, but the way of the wicked will perish." This same theology is the basis of hope in Psalm 7.

The psalmist portrays God's opposition to the evildoers in two different ways. One is that of a shield (7:10). This is the language of protection, like that of God as the refuge for the psalmist (7:1). The other is that of a warrior who carries out a righteous judgment. Note the reference to a warrior's weapons in verse 12. In spite of threatening circumstances, the psalmist shows that he has confidence in God's judgment in human affairs and thus that God will vindicate him. This serves as an example and guide for believers of every age.

For Those Who Sing Psalm 7

God's righteousness is a major affirmation of this psalm. His judgment is something to be confessed as both good and active in the give-and-take of human endeavor. Evil and evildoers are shown to be insidious and their thwarting testifies that God is at work. There are circumstances in life in which we find ourselves victimized or oppressed. In such circumstances we are innocent recipients of malevolent activity. Of course, judgment for failures is also an experience of believing people, but the emphasis in this psalm is that the one who prays is not guilty. God is able to frustrate evildoers and to use their acts as self-generated judgment.

Andrew Dearman

I Take Refuge in the Lord

Psalm 7

Russell D. Scott

Russell D. Scott
Arr. M. L. Daniels & Russell D. Scott

Lord, You Are a Righteous Judge

Psalm 7

Mark Shipp

Mark Shipp
Arr. M. L. Daniels

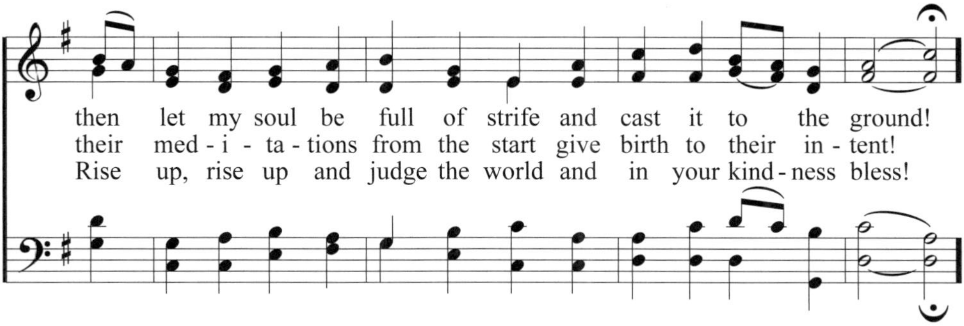
then let my soul be full of strife and cast it to the ground!
their med - i - ta - tions from the start give birth to their in - tent!
Rise up, rise up and judge the world and in your kind - ness bless!

Arise, O Lord, Deliver Me

Psalm 7

Mark Shipp

Michael E. Showalter
Arr. M. L. Daniels

Arise, O Lord, Deliver Me

PSALM 8

Translation

For the leader: according to The Gittith.[a] A psalm of David.

*1 O LORD, our LORD, how great is your name in all the earth! You have set your glory above the heavens.

†2 From the mouths of babes and infants you have established strength, because of your foes, to bring enemy and avenger to halt.

†3 When I look toward your heavens, the work of your fingers, the moon and the stars that you set up;

*4 what are human beings that you are mindful of them, mortals that you care for them?[b]

*5 Yet you have made them a little lower than God[c] and crowned them with glory and honor.

†6 You have given them responsibility over the works of your hands; you have put all things under their control,

†7 all sheep and oxen, and also the beasts of the field,

†8 the birds of the air, and the fish of the sea, whatever makes its way in the seas.

*9 O LORD, our LORD, how great is your name in all the earth!

[a] An obscure, possibly musical term, which may relate to a musical instrument (possibly from the town of Gath), or a tune, a festival, or individual perhaps from Gath.

[b] The Hebrew text has singular nouns, which can be translated more literally as "man" and "mankind" for the "human beings" and "mortals" provided above.

[c] The Hebrew word, *elohîm*, can be translated "God," "the gods," or "divine beings."

Structure and Poetry

This is a classic hymn of Israel, poetically structured with a coordinated beginning and end, which praises God as LORD of all. Praise of God as creator and sustainer is the substance of the hymn. It was almost certainly chanted and perhaps put to music in ancient Israel. Psalm 8 appears related to the narrative of the sixth day and the creation of man and woman in Genesis 1:26ff. Possibly it is a poetic rendering of the sixth day account and the creation of man and woman in God's image.

The basic structure of the Psalm is as follows: Verses 1 and 9 form an *inclusio*, brackets of praise for the material in the middle. Verses 2–5 celebrate the dignity and position of humans in the created order, and verses 6–8 affirm human dominion over the created order.

Theology and Application

God is the sovereign maker and Lord of creation and the guardian of right order. Children are the sign of the continuing goodness of creation and its creator. Human beings are given an exalted place in the divine economy. It would be wrong, however, to read this as a license rather than privileged responsibility. The same is true of Genesis 1:26ff. There, man and woman are given responsibility to have children and to rule. That they were created in the divine image is a functional matter. They are to be fruitful and to rule as God's designated representatives in his world. The expression here in 8:5 ("a little lower than God") renders the same series of thoughts as Genesis 1:26. These are powerful thoughts when considering the place of human beings, generally speaking, in God's created realm. All people have privilege and responsibility; believers can rightly celebrate this as they worship the cosmic king and Lord of all.

Hebrews 2:5–9 is a Christological reading of this psalm in which Jesus, the incarnate Lord, is understood to be, for a while, a little lower than God (or the angels, as the Greek text has it in v. 5) in accomplishing God's will.

For Those Who Sing Psalm 8

Praise of the creator befits creation, whether it is the cry of a baby or the voice of God's people. "Majestic" describes God's name and character in bringing forth the world and its inhabitants. The poetry of the psalm reflects upon the grandeur of God at work in creating man and woman, blessing them, giving them an exalted place in creation's orders, and extending them tasks in creation (Gen. 1:24–31). Human beings are privileged by God with certain responsibilities in creation that they should carry out in faithfulness to him. The writer to the Hebrews notes that we do not always see things in subjection to human control, but we have seen Jesus, who is the divine word and the only human being to whom sovereignty ultimately belongs.

Andrew Dearman

O Lord, Majestic Is Your Name

Psalm 8

Mark Shipp

Mark Shipp
Arr. M. L. Daniels

O Lord, Our Lord

Psalm 8

Dedicated to Jack K. Dorman Sr.

Debbie Dorman / revised — Debbie Dorman / revised

Psalm 9

Translation

For the leader: according to Mut-Labben.*[a] *A psalm of David.

1 (א, *aleph*)[b] I will praise the Lord with all my heart; I will recount all your wonders.
2 I will delight and be glad in you; I will sing praise to your name, Most High.
3 (ב, *bet*) When my foes turned around, they stumbled and perished before you,
4 for you have done justly in my case; you sit enthroned, judging rightly.
5 (ג, *gimel*) You have rebuked the nations, you have vanquished the wicked; you have blotted out their name forever and ever.
6 (ה, *he*) The foes are finished forever; their cities you have uprooted; their memory has perished.
7 (ו, *waw*) The Lord is enthroned forever; he has established his throne for justice.
8 He judges the world with righteousness; he judges the peoples with rectitude.
9 The Lord is a stronghold for the battered, a stronghold in times of trouble.
10 Those who know your name trust you, for you have not forsaken those who seek you, O Lord.
11 (ז, *zayin*) Sing praises to the Lord, who is enthroned in Zion. Make known his deeds among the peoples.
12 For he who avenges those murdered remembers them; he does not forget the cry of the afflicted.

13 (ח, *het*) Be gracious to me, Lord! See what I get from those who despise me! You are the one who raises me up from death's entrance,
14 so that I may recount all your praises in daughter Zion's gates, that I may rejoice in your deliverance.
15 (ט, *tet*) The nations are stuck in the pit that they made; their own foot has been caught in the net they hid.
16 The Lord has made himself known, he has carried out justice; the wicked are trapped in the work of their own hands. [*Higgaion.*[c] *Selah.*[d]]
17 (י, *yod*) The wicked will end up in *Sheol*, all the nations who forget God.
18 (כ, *kaph*) But the needy shall not always be forgotten, nor will the hope of the poor perish forever.
19 Rise up, Lord! Don't let mortals prevail! May the nations be judged before you.
20 Lord, give them reason to fear! Let the nations know that they are only human. [*Selah*]

[a] The function of *Mut-Labben* is obscure. It may be a tune. Its meaning is likewise obscure. Literally, it may mean something like "death of the son," or "death to the son," but the reference is unclear.

[b] Psalm 9 is an alphabetic acrostic (see below), with almost every other verse beginning with the successive letter of the Hebrew alphabet. The acrostic breaks down in several ways: it is missing the *d* line (*dalet*), there are four verses which all begin with the *w* (*waw*), and the psalm ends with the letter *k* (*kaph*). Psalm 10 picks up most of the rest of the acrostic with *l*. See commentary below and on Psalm 10.

[c] See below. The meaning of *higgaion* is obscure, but is also found in Psalm 92:3, where it is a musical term.

[d] See below and the translation note on Psalm 3 for *selah*.

Structure and Poetry

Psalm 9 is comprised of elements of praise for God as a righteous judge, along with requests, even pleas, that God govern accordingly in the face of opposition. Portions of the psalm are an acrostic, where the initial word of a verse begins with successive letters of the Hebrew alphabet, although the pattern is not carried out consistently. Also, some translations (and reading traditions) have seen Psalms 9 and 10 together as one composition. This is the reason why the Greek translation of the Psalter from this point onward is one number off. It takes the two psalms together, so that what in Hebrew and English is Psalm 11 is Psalm 10 in Greek, and so forth.

Verses 1–12 offer praise to God for his prior protection and thwarting of evildoers. Verse 10 nicely catches the sense with the confession that those who know the Lord's name trust him and have reasons to do so. Verses 13–20 present the circumstances of the psalmist before the Lord, beginning with a plea to the Lord for grace and concluding with a plea that the Lord put the nations in their proper place before himself.

There is evidence of the psalm being performed with music and/or chanting. In verse 16 are two terms, *higgaion* and *selah*, which are likely associated with cues for performance, even though their precise functions are unknown. *Selah* is also used at the conclusion of the psalm.

Theology and Application

The Hebrew term for justice/judgment is used as a noun and as a verb to describe the work of the Lord: he is a judge who acts on behalf of right and those in need of vindication. He stands over against the forces of evil and his righteous acts are on behalf of those who are oppressed or victimized by evil. The perpetrators can be individuals or nations, for both can and do oppose God and God's people.

In the case of evil perpetrators, God's judgment can take several forms. Sometimes the work of the wicked is self-destructive. That is the claim of verse 16. God oversees the process of their destruction. He works through the historical process to defeat the psalmist's enemies, since their persecution is at the same time opposition to God's servant. That is the claim of verses 3 and 5. God avenges the blood of the righteous and those who are oppressed because of their service to him. That is the claim of verses 11–12. Perhaps it is helpful to remember here the account of Cain and Abel in Genesis 4:1–16. When Cain murdered Abel, the Lord confronted Cain and told him that the blood of his brother cried out from the ground (Gen. 4:10). The prayer of Psalm 9 is also a cry to God, who knows the circumstances of the wronged.

For Those Who Sing Psalm 9

God is celebrated as a righteous judge and called upon to continue acting justly and upholding the weak and needy. The psalmist, too, is in need and promises to recount the greatness of the Lord. Giving testimony to God's greatness is one avenue of praise. The psalm is realistic about the power and presence of evil. Thankfully, evil ones do not have the last word, although their influence sometimes seems overwhelming. God stands against evil and those who practice it.

Andrew Dearman

I Will Praise You, O Lord!

Psalm 9

Glover Shipp

Katelyn Horn

Give Thanks to the Lord

Psalm 9:1-10

Mark Shipp

St. Denio, a Welsh melody
from *Canaidu y Cyssegr* by John Roberts

Arise and Remember

Psalm 9:11-20

Mark Shipp — M. L. Daniels

He Does Not Forget the Cry

Psalms 9 and 10
an alphabetic acrostic

Jerry Shipp & Mark Shipp

Mark Shipp

He Does Not Forget the Cry

Psalm 10

Translation[a]

1 (ל, *lamed*)[b] Why, Lord, are you far away? Why do you hide yourself in troubled times?

2 In arrogance the wicked afflict the poor. May they be caught in their own traps.
3 For the wicked exalt their desires; greedy folk spurn the Lord.
4 The wicked say self-servingly, "God will not bother with it"; they think there is no God.
5 (מ, *mem*) They seem to prosper all the time; your judgments are away from them. As for their foes, they poke fun at them.
6 They say to themselves, "We shall not be moved from generation to generation; no evil will befall us."[c]
7 (פ, *pe*) Their mouths are full of cursing and deceit and oppression; on their tongues are trickery and iniquity.
8 (ע, *ayin*) They wait in ambush in settlements; from hiding places they murder the innocent. They keep watch for the vulnerable.
9 They hide themselves like a lion; they wait to ambush the poor; they grab them and drag them off in their net.
10 They crush their victims, and the helpless fall by their power.[d]
11 They say to themselves, "God has forgotten; his face is hidden, he will never see it."

12 (ק, *qoph*) Rise up, Lord! O God, lift up your hand! Do not forget the oppressed.
13 Why do the wicked reject God and say to themselves, "You, God, will not pursue the matter"?
14 (ר, *resh*) You do see! Indeed, you see trouble and grief, and you take matters into your hands. The helpless commit themselves to you; you are the orphan's helper.
15 (ש, *shin*) Break the arm of the wicked and evildoers! Pursue their wickedness until it is gone!

16 The Lord is king forever and ever; the nations shall perish from his land.
17 (ת, *taw*) You will hear the hope of the humble; you will strengthen their heart and listen to them,
18 to do right by the orphan and the oppressed, so that mortal foes may strike terror no more.

[a] This psalm lacks a superscription, or title. This, along with the continuation of the acrostic from Psalm 9 and its connection to Psalm 9 in the Septuagint, suggests that Psalms 9 and 10 may have originally been part of the same composition.

[b] The acrostic picks up from Psalm 9 with the letter *l* (*lamed*). The presence of an *m* verse is dubious at best in verse 5, but the *n* (*nun*) and the *s* (*samek*) are clearly lacking. The *ayin* (a silent letter) and the *p* (*pe*) are reversed

(vv. 7 and 8), the *tsade* (*ts*) is lacking, and *q* (*qoph*), *r* (*resh*), *sh* (*shin*), and *t* (*taw*) occur at the beginning of verses 12, 14, 15, and 17.

[c] The last clause is a paraphrase of a difficult text.

[d] The Hebrew text is obscure.

Structure and Poetry

Psalm 10 completes the acrostic begun in Psalm 9 (see text note above and notes to Psalm 9; compare with the Greek translation of Psalms 9–10, a single psalm in the Septuagint). The psalm has basic components of the lament or plea to God: direct address and the plaintiff's requests to God (vv. 1, 12–15), description of the circumstances of oppression/affliction (vv. 2–11); and expression of confidence in God (vv. 16–18). An element that stands out in the first half of the psalm is the extended and vigorous description of evil and the wicked.

Theology and Application

The premise of the plea to God is that God hears and responds, even though sometimes he seems absent. This is a theme repeated many times in the Psalms and known to generations of faithful people. Even if answers to prayer are slow in coming or are not what we had hoped, there is encouragement to name evil for what it is, and to pray and to acknowledge that God does hear and act. The many psalms of lament are scriptural evidence that honest words of pain and questioning are not an exercise in futility. This psalm is a sobering reminder of the breadth and depth of evil and of widespread opposition to the standards of the creator. It contains the voice of realism as well as hope. The psalmist understands God as someone who takes the side of the weak, the afflicted, and the wronged. Without him many would be lost and consumed by those more powerful than they. God is the cosmic king (v. 16), defender of the needy in his realm, and the one who will vanquish the rebellious nations, even though their power at times seems overwhelming. This too is a theme among the prophets. God will judge the wicked because he is righteous and he will vindicate the poor and needy because he is compassionate.

For Those Who Sing Psalm 10

How easy it is to be overwhelmed by the power of evil and our own insecurities about the future, and then to doubt God's role in that future. It is part of the human condition to feel the absence of God. Think of Jesus' own citation of Psalm 22 in this regard. One of the wonderful things about the Psalms is that we can bring our feelings to the LORD. Frank language is no barrier to relating to God. Taking evil seriously means that the believer must also take seriously God's call to name and to oppose evil. Cries for help and relief only make sense if God does, in fact, hear and respond. A psalm like this one is based on the conviction that God responds to those in need and under threat.

Andrew Dearman

Why Do You Stand Far Off, O Lord?

Psalm 10

Mark Shipp

M. L. Daniels

Where Are You, Lord?

Psalm 10

Glover Shipp

Glover Shipp
Arr. Ruth Ann Somervell & M. L. Daniels

Psalm 11

Translation

For the choir director. A psalm of David.

†1 In the Lord I have sought refuge; how can you say to me,[a] "Flee as a bird to your mountain!

†2 For, behold, the wicked bend the bow, they make ready their arrow upon the string, to shoot in darkness at the upright in heart.

†3 Indeed, the foundations are being destroyed; what can the righteous do?"

*4 The Lord is in his holy temple; the Lord's throne is in heaven; his eyes see, his eyelids test the sons of men.

*5 The Lord tests the righteous,[b] but the wicked and the one who loves violence his soul hates.

*6 Upon the wicked he rains down coals of fire and brimstone, and burning wind will be the portion of their cup.

*†7 For the Lord is righteous; he loves righteousness. The upright will behold his face.

[a] Literally, "to my soul." The "you" could be a well-intentioned friend or simply the psalmist's own mind or heart.

[b] The Hebrew allows a reading that the Lord's testing could include the wicked, but the emphasis in the verse as a whole is on the testing of the righteous.

Structure and Poetry

This psalm is an individual song of confidence in two parts, set up by the question in verse 3b: "What can the righteous do?" The opening lines (vv. 1–3) set the situation. "In the Lord I have sought refuge," suggests that the psalmist had come to the temple in his time of crisis only to have either companions or an inner voice of fear question the very security of the temple as a refuge when its foundations have already been destroyed. Despite the futility of his question in 3b, somehow his confidence in the Lord is restored and he responds in verses 4–7 with a resounding affirmation.

In verses 1–3, two opposing positions are delineated: the faithful trust in the Lord, while the wicked mock them for a false sense of security. Verse 3 asks what one is to do when everything falls apart. The question, very simply but appropriately, leads to a definitive description of what it means to seek refuge in the Lord.

The righteous, in verses 4–7, trust in the Lord especially when things seem beyond God's control. Yet, the holy reign of the Lord from his temple stands securely against the violent attacks by the wicked. Their downfall is as certain as God's love for the righteous. The upright maintain this vision.

The psalm moves from a genuine, rather than a rhetorical, question, to a confident statement about true righteousness resting in the reign of the Lord, to a solid theological affirmation about real security.

Theology and Application

This psalm, usually classified as a personal lament, seems more fittingly to be a song of confidence sung in the midst of a crisis. Its theological center is the reality of the Lord's holy reign in the temple and in heaven (v. 4). This is the first of several affirmative doctrines sung in response to the question, "What can the righteous do?" Although "the wicked" are mentioned four times, "the righteous" or "righteousness" is used five times. The division, established in Psalm 1, between the righteous and the wicked continues in Psalms 2–11 with the Lord's preference for the former and sure judgment against the latter clearly seen in this psalm.

Additionally, Psalm 11 directly challenges the assumption of the wicked that their deeds are hidden from the Lord's view (v. 13) or that God does not exist (v. 4). The Lord's kingship, though not directly mentioned in this psalm, is elsewhere characterized by righteous justice that flows from his holy temple (Pss. 46–48; 93–99). There are numerous psalms that speak of the Lord as a refuge, but few are as focused as Psalm 11 on the Lord's defense and protection for the righteous who seek shelter in his holy abode.

When things seem to be falling apart around us, this psalm instructs us to ask, "What can the righteous do?" The overwhelming answer from this psalm is to trust in the Lord, no matter how bleak life may be. The Lord is our secure refuge, even when all else is collapsing.

For Those Who Sing Psalm 11

When quiet confidence in God collapses because the wicked seem to prosper, the psalmist asks what to do, since even the foundation is falling apart. Psalm 11 affirms that the righteous trust in the Lord in the midst of personal crisis, especially when things seem beyond even God's control. However, the holy reign of the Lord from his temple stands securely against the violent attacks of the wicked.

Craig Bowman

In the Lord Do I Take Refuge

Psalm 11

Mark Shipp

Mel Witcher

In the Lord Do I Take Refuge

In the Lord I Find My Refuge

Psalm 11

Mark Shipp

Kathy Thompson

In the Lord I Find My Refuge

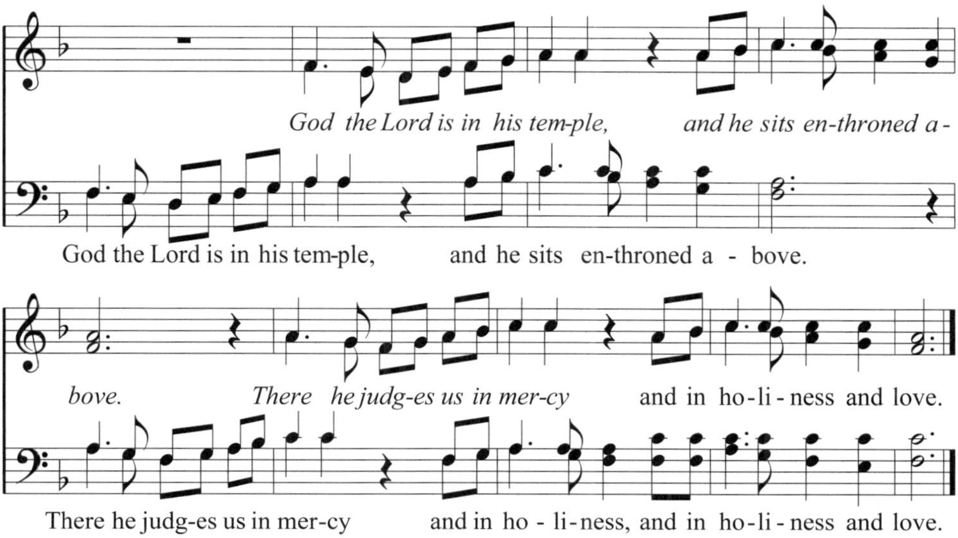

Psalm 12

Translation

For the choir director; upon an eight-stringed lyre.[a] A psalm of David.

[1] Help, O Lord, for the loyal one ceases to be, for the faithful disappear from among the
sons of men.
[2] They speak deceitful lies to one another; with flattering lips and with a double heart
they speak.

[3] May the Lord cut off all flattering lips, the tongue that speaks great things,
[4] who have said, "With our tongue we will prevail; our lips are our own; who is lord
over us?"

[5] "Because of the devastation of the afflicted, because of the groaning of the poor, now I
will arise," says the Lord. "I will set him in safety; I will shine forth for him."[b]
[6] The words of the Lord are pure words; as silver tried in a furnace on the earth, refined
seven times.
[7] You, O Lord, will keep them; you will preserve him from this generation forever.
[8] All around the wicked strut about, as vileness among the sons of men is exalted.

[a] The Hebrew says, "according to the *shemînîth*," or "upon the *shemînîth*." Suggestions for the word's meaning include an instrument of eight strings; the eighth string of an instrument; a lower octave than that indicated in 1 Chronicles 15:20; or the eighth day of a festival. Any of these meanings is possible. See also Psalm 6:1, 12:1, and 1 Chronicles 15:21.

[b] The Hebrew is uncertain and can mean "he will puff for it/him." This translation assumes a correction based on Greek and Syriac versions. See Psalm 94:1.

Structure and Poetry

This psalm probably functioned as a communal lament, though there are internal ambiguities with some singular pronouns and references. The *Opening Plea* for the Lord to save is followed by a simple *Complaint* about the disappearance of those who are loyal and faithful and the exaltation of those who speak flattering deceit (vv. 1–2). Next is an *Imprecation*, or curse, in verses 3–4. A *Salvation Oracle* is introduced with a motivational clause—the Lord has heard the outcry of the afflicted and poor (v. 5). Finally comes a string of *Affirmations* that rest on the purity of the Lord's speech in contrast to the empty words of the wicked.

The effective use of repetition and contrasting types of speech (human and divine) form the basis of this appeal for the Lord to save. Imagery related to speech abounds:

lips, tongue, boasting, groaning, and words. The purity of the LORD's words is demonstrated by the smelting of silver seven times, a perfect number.

In verses 1–4, a genuine plea for help is made on behalf of the godly. The speech of the wicked is a transparent indicator of their character, as lips and tongue reveal the heart. They boast in the strength of their words that seem to prevail to their advantage in all circumstances. These detractors disdain the LORD's sovereignty and relish in their self-perceived independence.

Prayer becomes prophecy in verse 5, as the LORD arises to save. This is a judicial metaphor frequently used in the Psalms (Pss. 3:7; 7:6; 9:19; 10:12; 17:13; 44:16; 59:4; 68:1; 74:22; 76:9; 94:1). What the Israelites first learned by the experience of rescue from Egyptian bondage (Exod. 2:23–24; 3:9–10), what they had been taught through Torah (Exod. 22:21–24), and what their prophets preached (Isa. 3:13–15), the psalmist remembers. The LORD's justice will be served. The word for safety (in salvation) is related to the cry for help (save) in verse 1; the prayer of the afflicted is fully answered.

In a dynamic contrast to the speech of the wicked, the word of the LORD is pure, dependable, and powerful (v. 6). His true word exposes the self-professed autonomy of the impious to be merely a thin shroud of talk.

In verses 7 and 8, the affirmation of the LORD's sustaining and preserving intervention resonates with his response in verse 5. The final line echoes verse 1, but the LORD has heard the appeal for help and entered to rescue from danger those who are loyal to him.

Theology and Application

Psalm 12 begins with an abrupt cry for divine rescue and then explains why. The good are being swallowed up by the words of the wicked. Evil is depicted here through speech, not deeds. The wicked speak smooth-sounding words without substance that threaten the well-being of those loyal to the LORD. Finally, the LORD hears the cry of the afflicted and is stirred to action, but the LORD's place of salvation is tied to his pure words. None of those words is spoken or quoted in the psalm, but the psalmist observes their effect and promises them for those who remain loyal. The LORD answers the prayer uttered in verse 1. The LORD's declaration to shine forth is a metaphorical description of his justice shining like the morning rays of the sun that dispel the darkness of the night (Ps. 94:1–7). The pure light of the LORD's words will penetrate the wicked world of darkness and injustice where the afflicted are devastated and the poor groan in agony.

The community of the faithful is often slandered by evil words spoken by those opposed to God, who claim accountability to no one but themselves. As the people of God, however, we live solely by the Word of God and trust in God's justice to deal with evil, even the words of the wicked.

For Those Who Sing Psalm 12

Psalm 12 complains that the words of the wicked wound the righteous, who voice their dilemma to God. In a dynamic contrast to the speech of the wicked, the LORD is pure, dependable, and powerful. The LORD rises to action, rescues the righteous, and brings justice.

Craig Bowman

I Will Arise

Psalm 12

Gary Pendergrass

Gary Pendergrass

Where Is the Faithful One?

Psalm 12

Mark Shipp M. L. Daniels

Psalm 13

Translation

For the choir director. A psalm of David.

[1] How long, O LORD? Will you forget me forever? How long will you hide your face from me?
[2] How long shall I take counsel[a] in my soul, *having* sorrow in my heart all the day? How long will my enemy be exalted over me?

[3] Consider *and* answer me, O LORD, my God; enlighten my eyes, lest I sleep the *sleep of* death,
[4] Lest my enemy say, "I have overcome him," *lest* my adversaries rejoice when I am shaken.

[5] But I have trusted in your loyalty; my heart shall rejoice in your salvation.
[6] I will sing to the LORD, because he has dealt bountifully with me.

[a] The RSV translates "pain," parallel to "sorrow" in the second half of the verse, rather than the Hebrew "counsels."

Structure and Poetry

This classic psalm of lament begins with an *Initial Plea* or *Invocation* that includes the *Complaint* proper (vv. 1–2). Next comes the *Petition* (or *Prayer*) with its *Motive Clause* (vv. 3–4). Finally, the psalm concludes with an *Affirmation of Confidence* and a *Vow of Praise* (vv. 5–6).

The fourfold repetition of the haunting phrase "How long?" in the first two lines accentuates the prayer of petition that follows. The strength of the prevailing enemy is matched by the psalmist's continued confidence in the LORD's loyalty and anticipated salvation and the psalmist's vow to praise. The four-time repetition also emphasizes the desperate state of the psalmist. The intensity of each phrase seems to rise, suggesting a real sense of neglect and abandonment by God, who may have intentionally turned away in judgment. Whatever the reason for the LORD's absence, it has produced a season of sorrow and agony reaching the point of death. The open-ended description does not allow determination of the precise situation.

Three strong and urgent petitions to the LORD (vv. 3–4) compel him to answer and act before the psalmist's life fades completely away. Without the LORD's intervention and strength, this person will surely die, with enemies or illness rejoicing.

In verses 5–6 the movement from pleas for help to successive petitions is anticipated; the movement from petition to affirmation and praise is, however, unexpected. Though shaken and despite desperate straits close to death, the psalmist's loyal commitment to the LORD remains. Remarkably, sorrow has not overwhelmed salvation and joy within his heart. It appears that his enemies were defeated, or his illness has been cured by verse six, when the psalmist sings to the LORD.

Theology and Application

Pain and grief, and the steady advance of death, choke out the psalmist's assurance that God is present and willing to save. The persistent questioning of the LORD's readiness to act, to remember, and to deliver creates a theological dissonance that is shockingly frank for believers. On the other hand, the holding together of complaint and praise teaches us about God and ourselves. The LORD comes through in the end and is involved even in life's worst moments. Such a conviction, as the internal coherence within this psalm demonstrates, prepares us for the unexpected worst that comes in life. The essence of life is relationship with God, so that threats to our existence are countered with remembrances of trust and anticipated praise.

For Those Who Sing Psalm 13

Pain and grief, and the steady advance of death, choke out the psalmist's assurance that God is present and willing to save. His persistent questioning of the Lord's readiness to act, remember, and deliver creates a dissonance that can be shocking for believers. On the other hand, the connection between complaint and praise teaches us about God and ourselves. The Lord comes through in the end and is involved even in life's worst moments.

Craig Bowman

How Long, O Lord, Will You Forget?

Psalm 13

Mark Shipp M. L. Daniels

How Long?

Psalm 13

Norman Horn

Katelyn Horn
Arr. Katelyn Horn & M. L. Daniels

Psalm 14

Translation

For the choir director. A psalm of David.

1 The fool has said in his heart, "There is no God." They are corrupt, they have committed
abominable deeds; there is no one who does good.

2 The Lord has looked down from heaven upon the sons of men, to see if any act pru-
dently, any who seek God.

3 They have all turned aside; together they have become corrupt; there is not one doing
good, not even one.

4 Do not all the workers of wickedness know, who eat up my people *as* they eat bread,
and do not call upon the Lord?

5 There they are in great dread, for God is with the righteous generation.

6 You would put to shame the counsel of the poor, but the Lord is his refuge.

7 Oh that the salvation of Israel would come out of Zion! When the Lord restores his
captive people, Jacob will rejoice, Israel will be glad.

Structure and Poetry

This psalm divides nicely into two sections: *Wisdom's lament* in verses 1–6 and a *Song of Salvation* in verse 7. It is a psalm of communal instruction, rather than a lament.

Poetically, a theological counter-affirmation follows observations about the foolish and corrupt whose moral orientation in life excludes God, as if he were not real. Some of these are immediate, coming right after the line stating the observation; other times an accumulation of observations is made before the counter line is offered.

In verse 1, the use of the word "fool" is a moral judgment of one who refuses to acknowledge God and lives accordingly. This amounts to pragmatic atheism where moral absolutes and divine accountability do not matter. In essence, the foolish are the wicked who practice social anarchy as if they were totally autonomous.

The Lord, as the sovereign creator, searches for the wise who seek him (v. 2). The pursuit of God differentiates humanity into two groups, the foolish and the wise. It manifests itself in personal trust (9:10), worship (22:26–27), and secure refuge (34:8–10).

Once again, in verse 3, the fool is described as being astray, corrupt, and evil. Not one of the foolish rises above his perverse nature.

In 14:4–6, God is with his people, the righteous and the poor, though they are devoured by the foolish/wicked. There is too little here to specify a stratified class-tiered society. Whatever the case, God will act on behalf of those who belong to him, providing safe haven and forcing the wicked into terrified respect.

The song of salvation heralds the LORD's restoration of his once captive people (v. 7). Mention of Zion certainly invites a connection with Jerusalem and the temple (Pss. 14:7; 50:2; 53:7; 110:2; 128:5; 134:3; 135:21; Isa. 2:3; Jer. 9:18; Joel 4:16; Amos 1:2; and Mic. 4:2).

Theology and Application

Psalm 14 states observed truths about the majority of humanity who seem to manage life without recognition of God's presence, purpose, or providential care. Though they are subject to his gaze and punishment, the foolish disdain any acknowledgement of the LORD's existence. The righteous, however, who seek the LORD, find refuge and hope of salvation through him.

Culturally speaking, we are in an age where most people live as if there were no God. There is, however, a righteous remnant that acknowledges the goodness of God and seeks his refuge. Often the remnant seems small and insignificant against the sinfulness of the world. However, as this psalm affirms, the LORD will bring salvation yet again to those who trust in him.

For Those Who Sing Psalm 14

Psalm 14 observes the truth that the majority of humanity seems to manage life without recognizing God's presence, purpose, or providential care. Though they are subject to his gaze and punishment, the foolish disdain any acknowledgement of the LORD's existence. The righteous who seek the LORD, however, find refuge and hope of salvation through him.

Craig Bowman

Come, Salvation, Out of Zion

Psalm 14

Marva L. Hughes | Marva L. Hughes

The Fool Has Said, "There Is No God"

Psalm 14

Mark Shipp | Kathleen Kirkland-Kanewske

The Fool Has Said, "There Is No God"

Psalm 15

Translation

A psalm of David.
*1 O Lord, who may abide in your tent? Who may dwell on your holy hill?

†2 Those who walk blamelessly, and do what is right, and speak the truth from their heart;
†3 who do not slander with their tongue, and do no evil to their friends, nor take up a reproach against their neighbors;
†4 in whose eyes the wicked are despised, but who honor those who fear the Lord; who stand by their oath even to their hurt;
†5 who do not lend money at interest, and do not take a bribe against the innocent.
* Those who do these things shall never be moved.

Structure and Poetry

This psalm, an entrance liturgy, divides nicely into three sections: Verse 1 articulates the *Entrance Questions* asked by the priestly Torah keepers of those approaching the entrance of the temple; verses 2–5b are the *Response* given by the people entering; and v. 5c is the *Blessing*, or the affirmation of acceptance, pronounced over those who have answered correctly as they climb the steps to the sanctuary.

The opening question is doubly stated. The answer is tenfold with three positives (v. 2) followed by three negatives (v. 3); and then two positives (v. 4) and two negatives (v. 5). This tenfold structure is analogous to the Decalogue in principle and wholeness, although the correspondence is not close to the Ten Commandments. The balance, however, suggests that this was a list of moral conditions for the admission to worship, easy for the congregants to remember and recite.

"Torah keepers" are generally characterized by the behavioral terms mentioned in this psalm as necessary for entrance to the temple: blameless, righteous, truthful, honoring and honorable; in other words, those who obediently keep the Torah. It is a promise of stability for the compliant.

The function and setting of this little dialogue are highly debated. There is plenty of ancient evidence that it was the role of temple priests to question pilgrim worshippers about acceptable conditions for their entrance and the role of the pilgrims to respond. Deuteronomy 26 describes a dialogue between those who brought their first fruits to the LORD and the presiding priest. Verses 13–14 contain similar high moral standards as Psalm 15:

> Then you shall say before the LORD your God: "I have removed the sacred portion from the house, and I have given it to the Levites, the resident aliens, the orphans, and the widows, in accordance with your entire commandment that you commanded me; I have neither transgressed nor forgotten any of your commandments: I have not eaten of it while in mourning; I have not removed any of it while I was unclean; and I have not offered any of it to the dead. I have obeyed the LORD my God, doing just as you commanded me" (Deut. 26:13–14, NRSV).

Compare Jeremiah 7:1–11, Haggai 2:11–13, Zechariah 7:2–3, and Malachi 2:7–9 for further evidence of priestly instruction and gate-keeping. Among other Old Testament texts regarding temple gate-keeping responsibilities is 2 Chronicles 23:19, which excludes anyone unclean from approaching the temple for worship. Deuteronomy 23:1–4 excludes people with certain physical deformities and backgrounds from worship. Psalm 118:19ff has one speaker asking for entrance to the temple and another replying that the righteous shall enter through the gate of the LORD (see also Ps. 24).

The questions are rhetorical, with the expectation that, of course, all worshipers will know the answers, or quickly learn them as they are repeated in the liturgy. However, there is no way that the priest could know whether the entrant had really kept the high ethical ideals.

The structure of the psalm is clear: priestly question (v. 1) followed by the pilgrim answer (vv. 2-5). The answer is expressed first in positive language and then by negative norms before a concluding promise.

The opening questions, at first glance, seem to be directed to the LORD alone. They are, however, addressed to those who are entering the temple. The answer given, however, is complex. Three participles with objects describe socially good conduct. Two more follow in verse 4. Five negative statements define evil behavior. The negative phrases are more specific than the positive; but none goes directly back to the Ten Commandments. On the other hand, the conditions for admission appear to be *ten* in number and a confirmed inner grouping of positive and negative conditions. Thus, the tenfold structure is analogous to the Decalogue in principle and becomes didactic (instructional) in function.

Positive Conditions (v. 2)

1. walking blamelessly
2. doing right
3. speaking truth

Negative Conditions (v. 3)

1. no falsity (double heart)
2. no evil
3. no reproach (against a neighbor)

Positive Conditions (v. 4)

1. despise evildoers
2. swear to do good

Negative Conditions (v. 5)

1. no usury (high interest loans)
2. no bribery

In verse 1, the word "tent" is probably a reference to the temple on Mount Zion (in parallel with "holy hill," later in the verse), the LORD's chosen abode that symbolizes his holy presence. These questions imply that those who belong to the LORD may enter into his presence to worship.

The answer (vv. 2–5b), rather than stating requirements for those entering, is a portrait of one whose being conforms to God's very character by influence of his Torah. As God is blameless, righteous, faithful, and true, so too will be the community in worship before him.

In verse 5c, the psalm concludes with an affirmation and promise regarding the doers of God's word: they shall not be moved. Thus, they are established and secure and will not waiver in the face of chaos. When unfortunate circumstances and conflicting forces strike the righteous, the holy presence and power of the LORD in their midst will uphold their lives.

Theology and Application

Psalm 15 (and the similar Ps. 24) raises the paradoxical question of the proper relationship between worship and ethics. Must one be ethically pure in order to worship acceptably, or is worship a means of motivating, becoming, enabling one to ethical purity? Both are true. Preparation for worship illuminates the necessity of worship for the pure of heart. Failure to uphold the ten conditions requires divine forgiveness prior to worship, making the invitation to enter God's holy presence to worship him a privilege that cannot be taken for granted or exploited casually.

This psalm, at its core, echoes the prophetic claim of exactly what it is that God desires of the worshipper: justice, righteousness, knowledge, goodness, and loving loyalty. Purity of heart is the requirement and goal for those who come into the presence of God to worship. For Christians, this psalm presents a reflective inventory that sobers our hearts for worship.

For Those Who Sing Psalm 15

Psalm 15 explores the moral integrity of those who gather to worship God. The dialogue between priests and pilgrims, coming into worship, centers on the willingness of the worshipper to accept the ethical standard explicit to the covenant with the Lord. The grace of God enables those who would come into his presence to live up to that standard and to experience the moral transformation uniquely available in worship. The mystery of worship, and its transformative power, offers those who enter the opportunity to take to heart what they know with their minds.

Craig Bowman

Unshakable and Standing Firm

Psalm 15

Ben Witherington, III

Marva L. Hughes

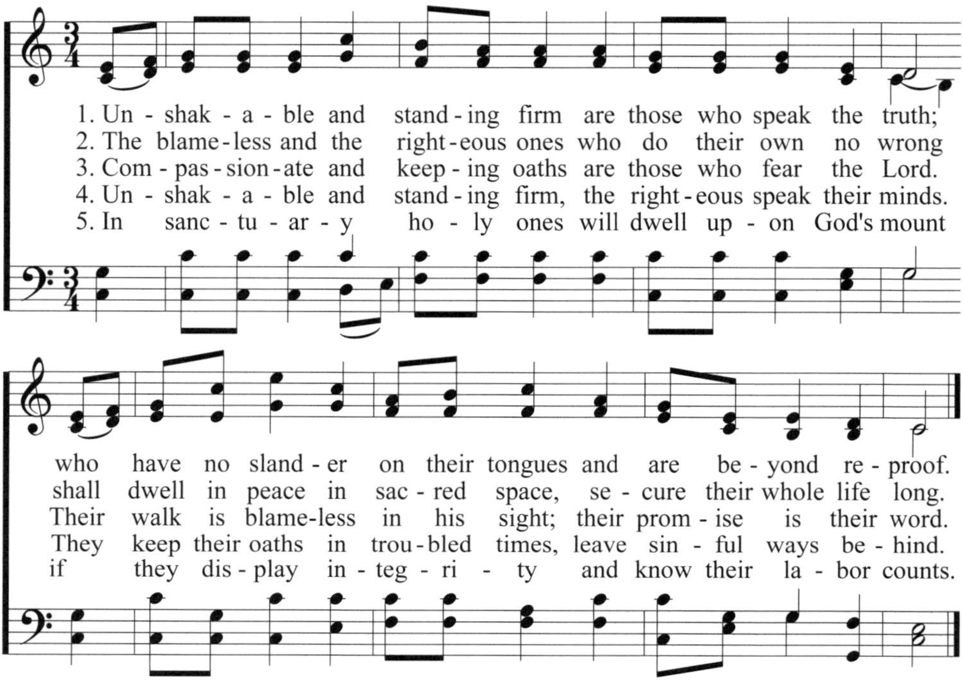

Who May Dwell?

Psalm 15

Jack R. Reese　　　　Jack R. Reese

Who Shall Abide?

Psalm 15

Mark Shipp

Mel Witcher

PSALM 16

Translation

A miktam[a] of David.

1 Keep me, O God, for I trust in you.

2 I said to the LORD, "You are my Lord. There is nothing good for me except you."

3 As for the saints who are in the land, they are the noble ones[b] in whom is my pleasure.

4 As for those who multiply idols, they hasten after another one. I will not pour out their drink offerings of blood, and I will not lift up their names on my lips.

5 The LORD is the share of my portion and my cup. You hold onto my lot.

6 Ropes have fallen for me in pleasant places; indeed, an inheritance pleasing to me.

7 I will bless the LORD who counsels me; also my inward parts[c] instruct me by night.

8 I always keep the LORD before me, so that at my right hand[d] I shall not be shaken.

9 Therefore, my heart rejoices and my soul[e] exults. Also, my flesh dwells in security.

10 For you have not abandoned my life to *Sheol*. You have not allowed your loyal one to see the pit.

11 You made known to me the path of life. Before you there is abundance of joy, and pleasant things are always in your right hand.

[a] The term *miktam* means something like "inscription." It is apparently similar to a *miktab*, an inscribed document or writing. It is found only in psalm superscriptions (see also Pss. 56, 57, 58, 59, and 60).

[b] Another translation option, though with some emendations of the Hebrew, would be, "As for spirits below and lords that others delight in, many shall be the troubles of those who turn back after them" (Eaton, *The Psalms* [London: Continuum, 2005], 96).

[c] Literally, "kidneys."

[d] Compare with RSV, "Because he is at my right hand..." Many versions add "he," though it is not present in the Hebrew.

[e] In verse 9, the Hebrew text reads, "and my glory rejoices," while the Greek text reads "and my tongue rejoices." One possible solution is to change the vowels of the Hebrew text to read "my liver" ("liver" and "glory" are similar in Hebrew). The Greek translators would have paraphrased one body part reference by referring to another. The liver, metaphorically, is the "heart" or the "soul."

Structure and Poetry

This psalm, like Psalm 17, expresses the desire of a lamenter to be in the presence of God. Whereas Psalm 17 is a lament of the individual, Psalm 16 expresses the trust that is both the precondition and the result of a lament.

The psalm's structure is:

Verses 1–4: Address and commitment of loyalty.
Verses 5–6: An expression of trust in God.
Verses 7–9: A commitment to praise God continuously.
Verses 10–11: Reasons for trust.

Theology and Application

The confession in verse 2 distinguishes the psalmist from idolaters. It also describes the benevolent nature of God in contrast to other potential views of the deity as capricious or dangerous. In verse 3, either the psalmist expresses commitment to the community of the faithful, or God is speaking and orienting the psalmist to the group to which he or she is to belong. Since Hebrew texts often switch speakers, either is possible. In any case, the psalmist does not live out his or her faith in a vacuum, but rather, in a community of like-minded and similarly acting persons. The first part of verse 4, and to some extent verse 3, is obscure. With the NRSV, I have taken the "holy ones" to be human beings, but the phrase often refers to angels or deities. If so, Eaton's translation in the notes above would be possible. In either case, the psalmist chooses to worship the LORD, rather than idols.

In verses 5–6, the psalmist has received what he or she needs to flourish. Ultimately, however, flourishing does not come from successful crops on fertile land, but from the God who gives fertility and life. Verse 7 refers literally to "kidneys," often paraphrased as "heart." The kidneys were considered to be the organ of affection and sentiment; they give the psalmist an awareness of the realities of life. In verses 10–11, *Sheol* is the realm of death, particularly for those who die in some unfortunate way, whether prematurely, painfully, or separated from family. *Sheol* is a symbol of the breakdown of human life; God has rescued the psalmist from the power of death, including the separation it involves from human society and the good aspects of human spirituality. To live in the community of faith is to escape death.

The psalmist expresses trust in God because God gives meaning, pleasure, and social connections in this life. God also advises humans on proper ways of living and is thus the source of wisdom (compare Job 28). The psalmist's trust is not merely mental assent, but a set of practices avoided or adopted: 1) proper worship (v. 4); 2) an openness to instruction (v. 7); 3) courage (v. 8); 4) and joy (v. 9).

The spirituality of joy, though only mentioned at the end of the psalm, is an important feature in biblical religion, especially connected with the festivals and the recitation of the mighty deeds of God (see Deuteronomy). Joy flows inevitably from trust in a benevolent God.

For Those Who Sing Psalm 16

Difficulties in life often challenge our faith. Yet the psalmist has learned that turning to God in trust and rejecting the shortcuts to security in life that tempt us all allows us to live with hope and confidence. He or she uses the images of death (*Sheol*) to describe the alternative he has rejected. Living in a trusting relationship with God leads to joy. At the same time, the existence of the psalm indicates the need to remind oneself of this joy and security, since neither the idols nor the drive for easy security that created them have disappeared.

Mark Hamilton

Secure Is My Heart, O God

Psalm 16

Glover Shipp

M. L. Daniels

Keep Me, O God

Psalm 16:1-3, 9, 11

Jack Boyd

El Cántico del Alba
California Mission Music

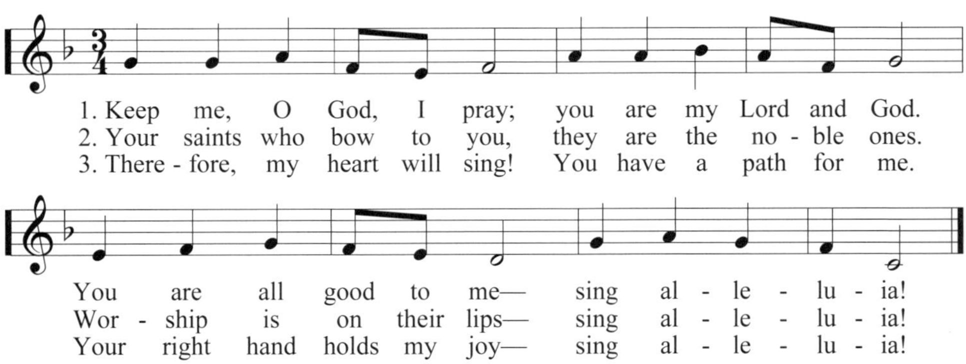

I Trust in You

Psalm 16

Randy Daw

Randy Daw

Psalm 17

Translation

A prayer of David.

1 Hear, O Lord, a just cause. Pay attention to my song. Listen to my prayer, rather than complaining lips.
2 May a judgment for me come from your presence. May your eyes see the right.

3 You have tested my heart, investigated it by night. You have smelted me and not found *anything*—an evil purpose will not pass my mouth.
4 For human actions, by the word of your lips, I have kept the paths of a bandit.
5 My steps cling to your tracks; my treads do not slip.

6 I called you, because you have answered me, O God. Stretch out your ear to me. Hear my utterance.
7 Show the marvel of your steadfast love, O Savior of the ones trusting in your right hand more than they fear their adversaries.
8 Keep me like the pupil of the eye; hide me under the shadow of your wings
9 from the wicked who pillage me; my enemies, who cut down my life from me.
10 They shut up the fat of their hearts; with their mouth they speak haughty things.
11 They now surround our steps; they look around for ways to cast *us* down to the ground.
12 They are like a lion itching for prey; yes, like a young lion lying in its hideout.
13 Arise, O Lord, face them and subjugate them. Rescue my life from the wicked by your sword,
14 from those who die—by your hand, O Lord—from those who die, whose lifespan, whose portion is in life. But as for your treasured ones, may you fill their bellies. May their sons have enough, and may they leave enough behind for their offspring.

15 I, by loyalty, will see your face. I will have enough just in seeing your visage, on awaking.

Structure and Poetry

This psalm is fairly difficult, with many textual variants and a few places in which the grammar is murky. The translation above follows the Hebrew text. I have tried to capture the jumps and starts in the text without smoothing over or paraphrasing them too much.

The structure is:

Verses 1–2:	Call for help.
Verses 3–5:	A protestation of innocence.

Verses 6–14: A renewed call for help (using a series of images of rescue).
Verse 15: An expression of trust.

Theology and Application

The psalm opens by asking God to listen to the content and intent of the prayer, not merely to the formalities of complaint. The psalmist is aware that others may complain for other reasons. Verse 2 focuses on the image of God as judge and defender of the innocent. Forming an *inclusio*, or "envelope structure," verses 3 and 15 mention the night. Perhaps the prayer is part of a ritual occurring at night in the temple. Such rites were commonplace in the ancient Near East (and many other cultures). A vigil before God oriented the one praying to the spiritual realities of ancient Israel.

Meanwhile, verses 4 and 5 take up other images, those of travel and highways (see also v. 11). The bandits seek back roads away from military garrisons and large towns, and thus the psalmist thinks of himself as cut off from normal human life. In verse 13, it is not clear who owns the sword because the ancient versions omit the pronoun "your" and thus interpret the sword as that of the enemies, from which the psalmist seeks protection. The grammar is awkward either way, and the translation adopted here seems to fit the Hebrew text slightly better. Verse 14 is also obscure. The second half describes God's providential care for the righteous, but the question is how part B relates to part A. Who are the "ones who die"? There are at least two options: 1) the "ones who die" are the enemies, in which case their fate is in contrast to that of "your treasured ones"; and 2) the "ones who die" are all human beings, in which case the phrase may have in mind the righteous, and their fate is the same as that of the treasured ones. It seems impossible to decide which meaning is correct, given the state of the text. However, it is safe to say that, for the "treasured ones," death does not pose a threat to their safety before God.

This psalm expresses the confidence those who seek to be righteous before God may have in God's protection and care. Although the world can be a threatening place, the religious community provides a location for prayer and thus for a reorientation to the true structure of reality under God's wings.

It is possible to live an ethical, spiritually vigorous life in the midst of adversity. The raw feeling of this psalm illustrates a form of spirituality that can exist in times of distress. The psalmist uses this prayer to reconnect himself or herself to the community of those praying. Prayer, not merely activities of various sorts, defines the community of believers.

For Those Who Sing Psalm 17

Security in God always exists in a dialectical relationship with the threats of evil persons and forces. The psalmist cries out to the delivering God for rescue. At the same time, he or she confronts the reality of evil, offering, in fact, an anatomy of the evil person as one whose intentions, actions, and commitments have all tended in a destructive direction. In contrast to them, the psalmist seeks God's provision of enough to live and the opportunity to see one's descendants. The psalm thus anticipates the stripped-down, but powerful, requests of the "Lord's Prayer" or "Our Father."

Mark Hamilton

Hear, O Lord, My Righteous Plea

Psalm 17

Glover Shipp | Konstantin Zhigulin

Rescue Me

Psalm 17

Keith Lancaster

Keith Lancaster

Rescue Me

1. En - e-mies sur-round me, throw me to the ground. Like a hun-gry li - on,
2. Lis-ten to my cry - ing, hear my right-eous plea. For my vin - di - ca-tion,
they have tracked me down. Show the won-der of your love; save me by your hand.
pray-ing you will see. Call - ing you to an-swer me, save me from my foe.
2nd time, D.C. al Coda
I have kept my heart for you; in your path I stand.
Their re - ward is in this life, mine in whom I know.
Lord. And I will see your face.

Psalm 18

Translation

For the leader. A psalm of David the servant of the Lord, who addressed the words of this song to the Lord on the day when the Lord delivered him from the hand of all his enemies, and from the hand of Saul.

1 He said: I love you, O Lord, my strength.

2 The Lord is my rock, my fortress, and my deliverer. My God is my rock in whom I take refuge, my shield and the horn of my salvation, my stronghold.

3 I called[a] upon the Lord, who is worthy to be praised; so I was saved from my enemies.

4 The cords of death encompassed me; the torrents of *belial*[b] overwhelmed me.

5 The cords of *Sheol* surrounded me; the snares of death confronted me.

6 In my distress I called to the Lord; to my God I cried for help. From his temple he heard my voice, and my cry for help reached his ears.

7 Then the earth shuddered and quaked; the foundations of the mountains trembled and shook, because he was angry.

8 Smoke went up from his nostrils and consuming fire from his mouth; glowing coals flamed forth from him.

9 He spread apart the heavens and came down, with cloudy darkness under his feet.

10 He rode on a cherub and flew; he soared upon the wings of the wind.

11 He made darkness his cloak, his canopy around him; thick clouds dark with water.

12 From the flashes before him burning hailstones broke through his clouds.

13 The Lord thundered in the heavens, and *Elyon*[c] uttered his voice.[d]

14 And he sent forth his arrows and scattered them[e]; he multiplied bolts of lightning and routed them.

15 Then the channels of the sea were exposed, and the foundations of the world were laid bare at your rebuke, O Lord, at the blast of the breath of your nostrils.

16 He reached down from on high; he took hold of me; he drew me out of mighty waters.

17 He delivered me from my strong enemy and from those who hated me, for they were too mighty for me.

18 They confronted me in the day of my distress, but the Lord was my support.

19 He brought me out to a wide-open space; he delivered me, because he delighted in me.

20 The Lord dealt bountifully with me according to my righteousness; according to the purity of my hands he rewarded me.

21 For I have kept the ways of the Lord and have not wickedly departed from my God.

22 For all his ordinances have been before me, and from his statutes I have not turned.
23 I have been blameless before him, and I kept myself from guilt.
24 So the LORD rewarded me according to my righteousness, according to the purity of
my hands in his sight.
25 With the loyal you show yourself loyal; with the blameless you show yourself blameless;
26 with the pure you show yourself pure; and with the twisted you are tortuously subtle.
27 For you deliver an afflicted people, but the eyes of the haughty you humiliate.
28 For you light my lamp; O LORD, O my God, you enlighten my darkness.
29 For with you I can run *against* a troop, and by my God I can leap over a wall.
30 This God—his way is blameless! The promise of the LORD is tried. He is a shield for
all who take refuge in him.
31 For who is God, except the LORD? And who is a rock besides our God,
32 the God who girds me with power and gives my way integrity?[f]
33 It is he who makes my feet like the gazelle's and makes me stand upon my crag.[g]
34 It is he who trains my hands for war, so that my arms can bend a bow of bronze.
35 You have given me the shield of your salvation, and your right hand has supported me;
your help has made me great.
36 You lengthened my stride under me, and my feet have not slipped.
37 I pursued my enemies and overtook them and did not turn back until they were finished.
38 I struck them down, so that they were not able to rise; they fell under my feet.
39 For you girded me with strength for the battle; you made my assailants bow down
under me.
40 You gave me the neck of my enemies, and those who hated me I annihilated.
41 They cried for help, but there was no one to save them. They cried to the LORD, but he
did not answer them.
42 I beat them fine, like dust before the wind; I cast them out like the mud of the streets.
43 You delivered me from the dissension of the peoples; you made me head of the nations;
people whom I never knew served me.
44 As soon as they heard of me they obeyed me; foreigners came cringing to me.
45 Foreigners fell and came trembling out of their strongholds.

46 The LORD lives! Blessed be my rock! May the God of my salvation be exalted,
47 the God who gave me vengeance and subdued peoples under me;
48 who delivered me from my enemies. Indeed, you exalted me above my adversaries; you
delivered me from the violent.
49 For this I will extol you, O LORD, among the nations and sing praises to your name.
50 Great deliverance[h] he gives to his king and shows loyalty to his anointed, to David and
his descendants forever.

[a] Many times in this psalm the Hebrew imperfect is used to describe completed action and is therefore rendered in the English past tense.

[b] Literally, "without worth," "worthlessness" or "wickedness."

[c] *Elyon* is usually translated "Most High."

[d] The repetition of "hail and fiery coals" in Hebrew may be due to dittography, or accidental repetition of words.

[e] The third person plural pronoun has as its antecedent "my enemies" in verse 3.

[f] The same Hebrew word (*tamîm*), translated "blameless," is in verses 23, 25, and 30.
[g] Literally, "upon my high place."
[h] The Hebrew word can also be translated "victories."

Structure and Poetry

This psalm is a royal song of thanksgiving structured around praiseworthy declarations of the Lord's character, using the central metaphor of a rock in verses 2, 31, and 46. These three verses stand out structurally as the backbone of the hymn. Between them are sections detailing the predicament of the psalmist who called upon the Lord (vv. 3–30), whose response is also described using a series of action verbs (heard, spread, rode, made, thundered, and uttered). In verse 30, a midpoint climax comes with the transitional assertion of three key concepts: the way of the Lord is blameless (vv. 21, 23, 25, and 32), the promise of the Lord (v. 50), and shield and refuge (vv. 2 and 35).

The second declaration of praise comes in verse 31, with a couple of rhetorical questions that focus on the incomparability of the Lord. Again the central metaphor of rock is repeated from verse 2. Verses 32–45 answer the rhetorical questions concretely by describing this God as the "God who . . ." Action verbs dominate the passage. The tables were turned dramatically and the former enemies cried for help to the Lord, but he did not answer.

Finally, the declaration of verse 46 brings closure to the hymn. It also reaches back to the metaphor of rock. Verses 46b–50 are simply a praise blessing that, growing out of verse 46a, summarize the whole of the psalm.

In verses 1–6, the opening phrase "I love you" is usually emended to "I exalt you" (compare v. 49). This line summarizes the point of the psalm. There is no question that God is the resource for the king's life and strength. Verse 2 enunciates more fully the completeness of this overarching statement. Although the metaphors are piled up, the central one of rock is used twice in this verse (four times in the psalm), emphasizing its particularity. Verses 3 and 6 reveal the time of trouble out of which the king cries. Death threatens to overtake him, but the enemies and circumstances are nonspecific. The presence of God, whether in his heavenly abode or in his temple on Mount Zion, is probably an intentional double meaning. The king is the Lord's chosen, as is Jerusalem/Zion.

Verses 7–19 use the language of *theophany*—earthquakes, smoke and flames, and the parting of the heavens—to announce God's hearing of the king's cry and his dramatic response. The Lord, in his anger, asserts his sovereignty by coming down to earth (v. 9). Moreover, his grand entrance is accompanied by lightning bolts and torrents of rain and hail designed to trap the king's enemies. His king, however, is plucked out of the raging storm and given royal shelter.

Divine justice and royal righteousness are interlinked in this section (vv. 20–30) suggesting that the king, who is completely dependent on the Lord, is exactly what God had in mind and empowered him to be. It underscores the reason for his deliverance given in verse 19c: "because he delighted in me." Mutual loyalty between the king and the LORD is celebrated.

The king's praise of the LORD (vv. 31–50) is in the form of a victory hymn. He begins with the incomparability of the LORD, the rock, who has equipped him with all gifts requisite of royalty. He is particularly grateful for the great act of deliverance and recent defeat of his enemies. While the king had a hand in the action, clearly the victory belongs to the LORD. The strength supplied to the king came from the LORD, and by this victory, he makes the king "head of the nations." His accomplishment ranges beyond his enemies, however, to lands and foreign peoples unknown. In effect, the shared victory between God and king not only places the king over all nations, but it also extends the LORD's sovereignty worldwide.

The three-fold structure outlined above, using the central metaphor of the LORD as rock, forms two semi-balanced sections devoted to the descriptive action of God. There are no literary devices used to create this, but the centrality of the incomparability of the LORD (v. 31) marks the midpoint, although it is not the perfect middle. Theologically, verse 31 dominates the whole.

Theology and Application

Verse 2, with its metaphors declaring the LORD as the king's savior, functions as a list of figurative synonyms for indexing the content of the psalm. The central metaphor of rock functions as the theological center for the psalm, capturing the psalmist's experience of distress and deliverance. The LORD is a safe haven during times of trouble and a high place for the king, who is likened to a sure-footed gazelle. The storm imagery is a physical description of the LORD advancing from the temple in Jerusalem to wild places, like En Gedi, where David hid from Saul. The LORD moves as in the midst of a thunderstorm, riding the wind and rain clouds, sending lightning, thunderbolts, and hailstones against the psalmist's enemies. But the psalmist himself must be sheltered from the stormy presence of the LORD as he aggressively scatters the enemy.

The hermeneutical challenge of this psalm is the appropriation of the triumph over personal enemies by the psalmist, who, with the LORD's help, pursues, overtakes, crushes, and subdues them. Christian use of the psalm moves more along the lines of the parallel imagery in Ephesians 6, with the shield of salvation as part of the whole armor of God used in spiritual warfare against the principalities and powers of this world.

For Those Who Sing Psalm 18

Psalm 18 declares emphatically the incomparable activity of God as deliverer, using the rich metaphor of a rock to symbolize his victorious might and superior strength. Though the rock image may at first seem to suggest God's passive and immobile response, this psalm recalls the dynamic deeds of God. It uses a broad collection of action verbs and related metaphors to describe what God does on behalf of the troubled psalmist. This leads the psalmist to celebrate the LORD's victory with declarations of praise for his faithfulness and covenant loyalty.

Craig Bowman

Choral

I Have Kept the Ways of Jehovah

Psalm 18:21-31

Jeff Matteson

Jeff Matteson

I Have Kept the Ways of Jehovah

I Have Kept the Ways of Jehovah

To the Faithful He Is Faithful

Psalm 18:20-36

Glover Shipp

M. L. Daniels

To the Faithful He Is Faithful

God of Integrity

Psalm 18:25-50

Debbie Dorman

Debbie Dorman

God of Integrity

Worthy Lord, I Give Praise to You!

Psalm 18:1-24

Felix Kneuper | Felix Kneuper

Worthy Lord, I Give Praise to You!

In My Distress

Psalm 18:1-19

Jeff Matteson

Jeff Matteson
Arr. M. L. Daniels

sum - ing fire came from his mouth. He rode the cher - ub on the
moun - tains trem - bled and they shook. One blast of breath re - vealed the
bolts of light-'ning round a - bout. In my dis - tress they had con-
wings of wind. The heav - ens rent and he came down.
o - cean depths, foun - da - tions of the earth laid bare.
front - ed me, but he de - light - ed in my life.
O Lord, my for - tress. O Lord, my strong - hold.
O Lord, my strong shield. O Lord, my Sav - ior.
O Lord, O, my strength. O Lord, O my rock.
1, 2
3
O Lord, my ref - uge.
O Lord, most high God.
O Lord, I love you. O Lord.

Psalm 19

Translation

For the director. A psalm of David.

*1 The skies recount God's glory, and the sky tells of his hands' work.

†2 Day announces a word to day, and night declares knowledge to night.

†3 No one speaks, no words exist, no voice of theirs is heard.

†4 Yet, their sound echoes through all the earth, their words to the dry land's end. He has put a tent in them for the sun.

†5 Yes, it is like a bridegroom going from his canopy, rejoicing like a warrior running down a path,

†6 from the end of the skies where it goes, making a circuit back to their end, so that nothing is hidden from its warmth.

*7 The LORD's law is perfect, refreshing the spirit. The LORD's counsel is certain, making the naive wise.

*8 The LORD's instructions are upright, making the heart rejoice. The LORD's command is pure, enlightening the eyes.

*9 The fear of the LORD is clean, standing forever. The LORD's judgments are true, doing justice in every respect.

*10 *All these things are* more precious than gold, than a pile of pure gold, and sweeter than honey, than drippings of the honeycomb.

†11 Also, your servant is warned by them. In keeping them is great reward. Who understands errors? Preserve me from unexamined faults.

†12 Also, hide your servant from arrogant persons.[a] May they not rule over me. Then, I will be innocent of serious sin.

*13 May my mouth's words and my heart's thoughts be pleasing to you, O LORD, my rock and rescuer.

[a] In verse 12, the Greek Septuagint reads "strangers," where the Hebrew reads "arrogant ones." I chose to read with the Hebrew.

Structure and Poetry

This psalm is fairly easy to translate and understand. Yet its intrinsic beauty and spiritual depth have made it a longtime favorite. The structure of the psalm is

Verses 1–6: The creation's praise of God.
  a. Verses 1–4b: A meditation on the creation's praise.
  b. Verses 4c–6: A digression on the sun's activity.
Verses 7–10: Humanity's praise of God.
Verses 11–13: The psalmist's petition for protection.

The apparent simplicity of this structure masks a very complex relationship of the various parts. As a Wisdom Psalm that shares the common view that human worship takes place in the context of all creation's adoration of God (see Pss. 104 and 147; Job 28 and 38), Psalm 19 begins with a meditation on creation's praise. It then moves to the human need for wisdom. What have wisdom and praise to do with each other? The human pursuit of truth, manifested in the study of Torah, takes place in the context of the spiritual formation of the believing community, which, in turn, is aware of, and sensitive to, God's overall care for the entire world. Thus the juxtaposition of the two parts of the psalm bears witness to deep spiritual assumptions that the psalmist is making.

Theology and Application

In verse 2, the combination of "speech" and "knowledge" sounds like the pursuit of wisdom. That is, the markers of time—day and night—engage in what is otherwise a human pursuit, the search for wisdom. Since time itself is seeking words and ideas that express the splendor of God, this activity must be woven into the very fabric of the universe itself. Such an activity does not derive from human nature, but from the nature of all creation. Wisdom is thus a gift of God and a property of the cosmos.

At the same time, according to verse 4, the psalmist is aware that the creation uses language differently than humans do. He or she explores the limits of the metaphors of verses 3–4. Verses 4c–6 continue the thought in a different direction. In the ancient world, the sun was thought to make a circuit around the earth, descending to the underworld during the night and reentering the visible world at dawn. These verses assume such a view. They take it in two ways, however: 1) the sun's circuit is an occasion of joy both for it and for those who witness it (comparable to that of a bridegroom); and 2) the sun's circuit allows it to see everything and to benefit everything. Incidentally, whereas in ancient Near Eastern texts the sun was a god and was often responsible for justice (hence the need to see everything), in this text it is merely a creature that proclaims God's glory.

The meditation on wisdom/Torah in verses 7–10 sounds a lot like the Proverbs. Here there are six synonymous statements climaxing in a general reflection on the preciousness of learning and the joy that comes from it. There are two sides to each statement: the "objective" side of the thing learned (law/decrees/precepts/commands) and the "subjective" side of its effects on the person learning.

Again, the psalm envisions the formation of an ethical, spiritual person who is in touch with all creation by means of Torah. Verse 9's "fear of the LORD" is the closest Hebrew equivalent to "religion." To be in awe of God is to be religious. Verses 11–13, the end of the psalm, take the reflections from the general to the deeply personal. The psalmist must turn his or her own heart to God in order to be blameless. These verses express several dimensions of spirituality: 1) the interior, private life; 2) morality; and 3) social aspects of life and faith. The last verse speaks of both the psalm itself, which the psalmist hopes pleases God, but more broadly, of all words and thoughts of which a religious person is capable. Unlike the skies and the days, human beings have the ability to turn language away from the praise of God and so must reflect on how we use it.

The modern tendency to downplay creation as a theological reality is alien to the thinking of this psalm. Far from being separate from other parts of reality, humans function as one with them. We have the same origins, purposes, and practices. Human spirituality should take that into account. The challenge for Christians in reading this psalm is to keep together sensitivity toward creation with the ethical demands of Scripture. For Jews in the biblical and post-biblical periods (until today), Torah provided a window into God's desire for order and purpose in human existence. Keeping Torah did not mean uncritical acceptance of rules, but an openness to the working of God in the lives of individuals and communities of faith.

For Those Who Sing Psalm 19

Like other biblical texts (for example, Pss. 1, 119; Prov. 8), this psalm connects human wisdom to the beauty and order of creation. The psalmist celebrates the exquisite beauty of the world, singling out the most beautiful creation of all, Torah. God's revelation gives direction to the lives of individuals and communities. Those who embrace Torah can experience the pleasure that comes from knowing that their lives are meaningful and part of God's intended order for all the creation.

Mark Hamilton

The Heavens Tell the Works of God

Psalm 19

Mark Shipp | Ruth Ann Somervell

More Precious than Gold

Psalm 19

Ruth Ann Somervell

Ruth Ann Somervell

More Precious than Gold

The Heavens and the Firmament

Psalm 19

Martha Pounders Walker

Jeff Matteson
Arr. Konstantin Zhigulin

Psalm 20

Translation

For the director. A psalm of David.

*1 May the Lord answer you in a day of distress. May the name of the God of Jacob lift you up.

†2 May he send you help from the sanctuary, and may he support you from Zion.

†3 May he commemorate all your gifts and pay attention to all your whole burnt offerings. [*Selah*]

†4 May he give[a] you what your heart desires and fulfill all your plans.

†5 May he rejoice in rescuing you when we set up banners[b] in our God's name. May the Lord fulfill all your requests.

*6 Now, I know that the Lord will rescue his anointed one. He will answer him from his holy heavens. With might shall his right hand save.

*7 These *trust* in chariots and these in horses. But we commemorate the name of the Lord our God.

*8 They bow down and fall, but we rise up and stand tall.

*9 O Lord, rescue the king. He will answer us in the day we call.

[a] Some ancient versions read "May the Lord give . . . ."

[b] Verse 5 also has a significant textual variant, for the Greek Septuagint, instead of "set up banners," reads "we have been glorified." It is difficult to decide which reading to prefer, though "set up banners" is more obscure and would more naturally have been changed to the easier "be glorified" than the other way around.

Structure and Poetry

This Royal Psalm apparently began as a war hymn, seeking divine help for the ruler during battle. However, it became part of the comprehensive collection that is the Psalter in order to function as a more generic petition for divine guidance of the nation at all times. The structure of the psalm is:

Verses 1–5:	Benedictions for the king and nation.
Verses 6–9:	A response of trust.

Theology and Application

The benedictions open in verse 2 by recognizing that warfare involves suffering and hardship. The title "God of Jacob" reminds hearers that God has a history with Israel, a history of protection and care. Verse 3 highlights the temple because it is God's national dwelling-place. (For a meditation on the temple, see Ps. 84.) As the place at which God meets Israel in a special way, the temple in Jerusalem becomes a symbol in the religious imagination for God's universal protection and care for those who pray to him.

The idea of verse 4 is not that one can bribe God, but that the gifts one offers, if given in trust and gratitude, count in building the relationship between God and the one offering. Similarly, verse 5 does not turn God into a dispenser of goods and services. The God of the Bible cannot be manipulated as a source of power. That is, the line assumes that the praying person desires good things, not unworthy things.

Verse 7 marks a turn in the psalm, which probably implies a change of speaker or at least of the position of the speaker vis-à-vis the audience. Prayer rests in the confidence that God listens and cares. Verse 8 offers a peculiar line in time of war, but it is a recognition of the limits of ordinary means of military prowess (compare with Deut. 17:14–20). The vicissitudes of war render human preparations ineffectual, unless the divine warrior is on one's side.

The psalm seems at first to be a bid for divine help in warfare, quite apart from human morality or even religious faithfulness. Thus it should be placed in the context of all the Old Testament's discussion of warfare. However, the psalm seems to do much more than express nationalistic fervor, as verse 8 indicates. The Old Testament is concerned that Israelites not assume that their national ambitions are identical with the plans of God. Nor should they believe that God guarantees them victory regardless of their behavior. Rather, security is conditional upon ethical behavior. As part of spiritual Israel, the church does well to remind itself of the limits of divine sanctioning of its deeds and attitudes.

In this psalm there are strong elements of trust in the face of adversity that deserve our attention. The psalmist seeks God's help during a time of crisis. Psalms cannot give the ins and outs of political analysis. They can simply ask God for help. This psalm does so, without being very specific about results. Its very vagueness is an encouragement.

For Those Who Sing Psalm 20

We all face the temptation of trusting in our own skills and strengths while pretending to trust God. The psalmist cuts through these illusions to note that human power (chariots and horses) cannot ultimately deliver us from our most frightening enemies, since those foes lie within us. Only God can ultimately save. The psalm celebrates such a conviction even in a time of war, when the temptation to trust in human might is strongest, and when religion is most easily subverted by the powerful to serve selfish ends.

Mark Hamilton

May Jehovah Answer

Psalm 20

Marva L. Hughes

Marva L. Hughes

In the Day We Call

Psalm 20

Chant

Translation by Mark Hamilton

Ruth Ann Somervell

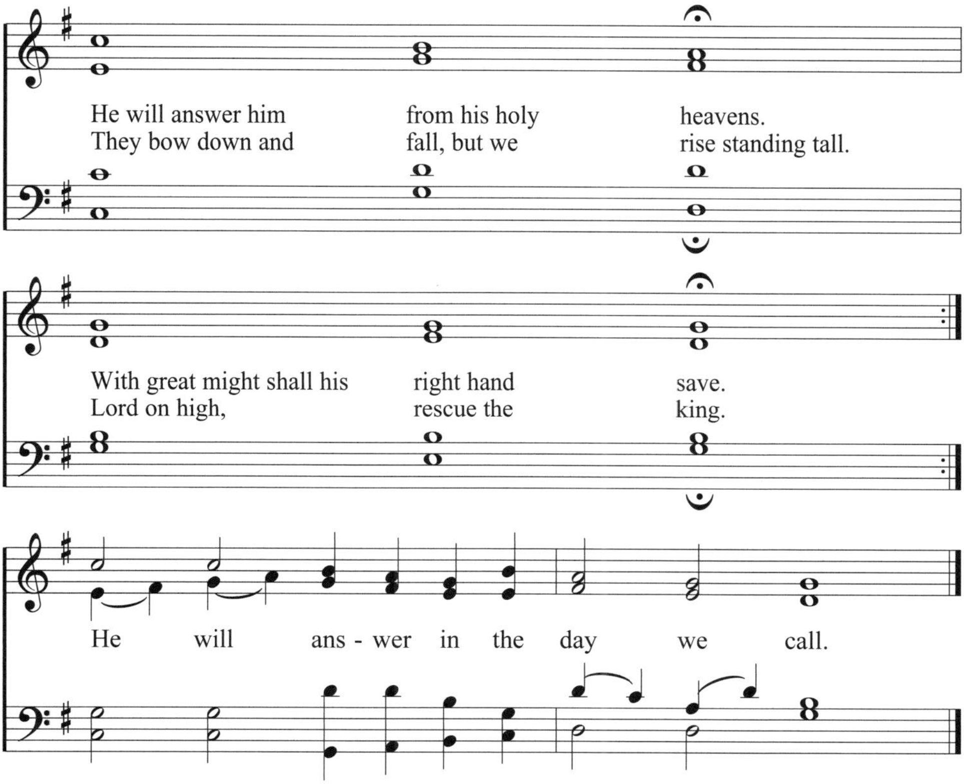
He will answer him from his holy heavens.
They bow down and fall, but we rise standing tall.
With great might shall his right hand save.
Lord on high, rescue the king.
He will ans - wer in the day we call.

He Will Answer

Psalm 20

Ruth Ann Somervell

Ruth Ann Somervell

He Will Answer

In the Day of Distress

Adapted from Psalm 20 and Numbers 6:25-26

Trans. Mark Shipp

Konstantin Zhigulin

Psalm 21

Translation

For the director. A psalm of David.

1 O Lord, may the king rejoice in your strength. And in your salvation, how much he
will celebrate!
2 You have given him his heart's desire, and you have not refused the request of his lips.
[*Selah*]
3 You make good gifts go in front of him; you put a golden crown on his head.
4 He asks life from you, and you give it to him—everlasting days, forever and ever.
5 His glory is great because of your rescue. You have placed on him splendor and majesty.
6 For you put before him everlasting gifts, and you made his face show joy.
7 For the king trusts in the Lord, and because of the Most High's loyalty, he will not quake.

8 Your hand will find all your enemies; your right hand will find those who hate you.
9 You will make them like a fiery furnace when you show your presence, O Lord. In his
anger, he swallows them, and fire devours them.
10 Their offspring shall perish from the earth, and their lineage from among human beings.
11 For they plotted evil against you. They conspired on a project they could not carry out.
12 For you have turned a shoulder to them, with your bowstrings pointed at their faces.

13 Arise, O Lord, in your strength. Let us sing and exult at your might.

Structure and Poetry

The psalm has a recognizable structure: the superscription; verses 1–7, a statement of the king's trust in God and the reasons for it; verses 8–12, an address either to the king or to God about victory over enemies; and verse 13, a final cry to God and a promise to praise. This psalm of praise is associated with warfare and probably with the king's coronation or his role at a major festival.

Theology and Application

Verse 2 addresses the king's role in the festival and the need of those in power to submit to something higher than themselves, namely God. For verse 2, compare the story in 1 Kings 3:4–15. The king must seek good things fit for his station as the guardian of the nation (see Ps. 101). The verse does not imply that God is at the king's beck and call, but rather the reverse. Verses 3–6 explain the meaning of verse 2. The survival of the dynasty meant the stability of the kingdom, ordinarily a good thing. Verse 9's "when you show your presence" is literally "at the time of your face," i.e. when the enemies see the face of God and thus experience terror and death because of their own sins. Verse 11 is reminiscent of Psalm 2, also a Royal Psalm, which portrays enemies of the monarchy as plotters and schemers. These psalms espouse a desire for justice and order in the land, not the abuse of power by either ruler or ruled.

In verse 12, "for you have turned a shoulder to them," is the best translation of several options. The LORD is an archer who has drawn his bow and adopted the stance for firing.

Verse 13's call to God is similar to those common in many psalms. The plea is that, since God has acted graciously and reliably in the past, the nation wishes to count on God's doing so again.

The last verse of the psalm raises two interesting paradoxes in biblical theology: God is both ever-present and sometimes seemingly absent. Humans count on God for help, but must ask for it. These seemingly contradictory truths together describe an important feature of reality, the fact that we know that God is always around, by definition, yet often seems absent. We are like the fish that forgets it swims in water. The cry to God is at the core of biblical faith, as will also be clear in Psalm 22.

It is tempting to think of this psalm as political propaganda. There is some truth to such a view, but the psalm is much deeper than this would allow. The Bible is often highly critical of both individual rulers and of power in general. Biblical authors routinely express deep suspicion of those at the top and their motives and plans. Thus we should put a psalm like this in the context of Israel's overall view of kingship, which is that those in power have great responsibility and must answer to God, who knows all and takes account of all, and who cares deeply for every single human being.

This song's view of kingship is expressed in verses 2 and 8: the king must trust God, rejoice when the innocent are rescued, and work to be part of God's overarching care for the world. This song does not celebrate raw power or allow itself to be hijacked for political purposes.

The psalm draws a sharp contrast between life, the realm of God, and death, the realm opposed to God. Throughout the Old Testament, God is portrayed as a God who brings life and all of the good things in it to human beings.

For Those Who Sing Psalm 21

This Royal Psalm promises victory for the king because he defends the good and opposes evil. The psalm reminds us that good and evil are ever-present realities. We must choose one or the other. Good will triumph when people choose it. Ultimately, it will triumph because God has chosen it.

Mark Hamilton

In Your Strength, Jehovah

Psalm 21

Marva L. Hughes

Marva L. Hughes

Be Exalted, Lord, in Strength

Psalm 21

Mark Shipp | Ruth Ann Somervell

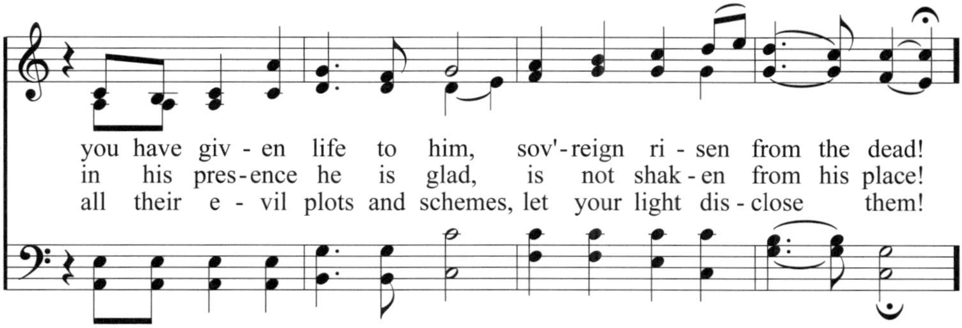
you have giv - en life to him, sov'-reign ri - sen from the dead!
in his pres-ence he is glad, is not shak - en from his place!
all their e - vil plots and schemes, let your light dis - close them!

Psalm 22

Translation

For the director. To the tune, "Fallow Deer at Dawn." A song of David.

†1 My God, my God, why have you abandoned me? My screaming words are far from *bringing about* my rescue.

†2 My God, I call out by day, and you do not answer; by night, and I never experience any silence.

*3 But you are holy, dwelling upon Israel's praises.

*4 Our ancestors trusted you. They trusted and you rescued them.

*5 They cried to you and were rescued. They trusted you and were not humiliated.

†6 But I am a worm, not a human being; a disgrace of a man, an embarrassment to the people.

†7 All who see me deride me. They curl their lip and shake their head.

*8 "Let him commit himself to the Lord; let him rescue him. He will rescue him, for his pleasure is in him."

*9 For you drew me from the womb, made me trust the breasts of my mother.

*10 On you was I cast from birth; from the womb of my mother, you were my God.

*11 Do not be far from me, for trouble is near, for there is no helper.

†12 Many bulls surround me; wild oxen from Bashan box me in.

†13 They open their mouths against me—a lion tearing and rending.

†14 I am poured out like water, and all my bones are dislocated. My heart is like wax, melting within me.

†15 My palate is dry as a shard; my tongue sticks to the roof of my mouth, and you commit me to the dust of death.

†16 For dogs surround me, an evil pack circles me, like a lion *would circle* my hands and feet.[a]

†17 I count all my bones. They stare; they gaze at me.

†18 They divide my clothes among themselves and cast lots over my garment.

*19 But you, O Lord, do not be far away. Hurry, oh my strength, to my aid.

*20 Rescue my life from the sword, my precious life from the dog's claw.

*21 Save me from the lion's mouth and deliver from the horns of the wild oxen.[b]

*22 I will recount your name to my brethren; in the middle of the congregation shall I praise you.

†23 "Those who fear the Lord, praise him! All the lineage of Jacob, glorify him! Be in awe before him, all the offspring of Israel!

*24 For he did not despise nor scorn the plea of the poor, nor did he hide his face from him. When he cried to him, he listened."
†25 My prayer is with you in the great assembly. I will perform my vows before those in awe of him.
†26 The poor will eat and have enough. Those seeking him will praise the LORD. May your heart live forever.
*27 All the ends of the earth will remember and turn to the LORD. Yes, all the families of the nations will bow down before you.
*28 For sovereignty belongs to the LORD, even rule among the nations.
*29 All the robust ones of the earth will eat and worship. All those going down to the dust, whose spirit will not revive, will bow before him.
*30 Offspring will serve him; it will be numbered to the LORD for generations.
*31 They will go forth and tell of his righteousness to people yet to be born, for he has acted.

[a] The Hebrew says, "Like a lion my hands and feet."
[b] The Hebrew says, "Then from the horns of the wild oxen you answered me."

Structure and Poetry

Like many psalms of lament, this one has a four-part structure: address to God (vv. 1–2); description of the psalmist's plight (vv. 3–18); a call for help (vv. 19–21); a promise to praise God interspersed with statements of praise (vv. 22–31). Laments also often have an expression of trust in God somewhere in the middle; verses 4–5 and 10–11 offer a modified version of one.

Theology and Application

The superscription may give the name of an ancient tune; no one today knows how it sounded. Verse 1 is among the most famous in the Old Testament as the one Jesus uttered on the cross when he joined the laments of all who feel God's absence. In this psalm, the one lamenting—who could be anyone—expresses grief at God's apparent indifference to his or her plight.

Verse 3 makes a metaphorical association: God sits on a throne; the throne is made up of the prayers of the people. Prayer is thus an act of enthroning God in the life of the community of Israel. Verse 4 makes the argument that God should listen to the lamenter, just as God had listened to all those who had prayed before. The people of Israel have addressed this God before and will confidently do so again. Verses 6–8 express the humiliation the lamenter feels. The very community which should be supportive ridicules him or her for trusting God. The verse is thus deeply ironic. The people who should believe in prayer and should support those in distress turn out to be the very ones who fail to do so. Verse 8 quotes those who mock the psalmist. Verses 9–10 make a second argument (the first was in v. 5). Since God was the lamenter's midwife, God should now care for the child thus brought into the world. The use of explicitly feminine imagery for the LORD is interesting. Some have thought this refers to a father acting as midwife, but this is not the most natural explanation.

In verses 12–21, the use of animal imagery gives a sense of terror and hopelessness to the lament. The lamenter feels like a hunted animal running to and fro for its life. Verses 17–18, also quoted in the Gospels in reference to Jesus' passion, here describe the vulnerability of someone whose poverty simply exposes him to the utter lack of compassion on the part of others. In verses 22 and 25, as often in Psalms of Lament, the lamenter promises to praise the LORD in the assembly of the people at festivals. Such occasions remembered not only God's saving acts in the past, but also provided examples of salvation in the present.

Verses 23–24 and 26 quote the actual words of praise that the lamenter speaks in the assembly. Other verses in this section may also be such quotations. God's protection of the vulnerable, the low in status, the sick, and the disenfranchised causes rejoicing in the community of Israel because it remembers its own history as an enslaved people. The psalmist demonstrates to God his or her commitment to praise by articulating extensive lines of praise even in the midst of the suffering that the psalm so brilliantly describes.

As verses 27–31 show, this psalm (like Ps. 24) thinks of God's universal rule, not just God's interest in Israel. Verse 30, meanwhile, contrasts the strong with the weak—all worship the God who delivers.

Lament is a popular form of psalm because biblical faith allows the believer to address God with every imaginable emotion, want, or word. God is not threatened by our most raw expressions of fear or anger as long as they are directed at him and come from a heart longing for healing. The honesty of the psalm deserves emulation in our own prayers.

The psalmist's distress has at least three dimensions. 1) It is internal, taking the form of deep psychological distress. 2) It is theological, for the psalmist has questions about the goodness or reliability of God. 3) It is social, for the psalmist experiences alienation from the community of Israel, even as he or she promises to return to that very community with words of praise. The mockers or enemies here are not foreigners, at least not necessarily so, but one's neighbors and friends. Yet those very persons will hear words of praise to God.

The psalm was apparently one of Jesus' favorites. It is not, of course, a prediction of the events of the Passion Week. Rather, Jesus prayed this psalm in order to join all the rest of us in our fear, sense of disorder, and longing for God's healing presence. Hearing him pray its words reorients us to the reality of our need for God and our need to identify with others in pain.

For Those Who Sing Psalm 22

Lament is a legitimate part of worship. In lament, we bring to God our most honest concerns, our fears, our sources of weakness, and, by implication, also our desire for alternatives. This psalm explores the depth of sorrow experienced by someone who has lost friends or meaningful occupations, or who doubts God's faithfulness. The psalmist feels abandoned, yet cries out to the one who has, seemingly, abandoned him or her. God hears the cry of those who seek deliverance. Such laments are not unwelcome in heaven because God seeks an honest relationship with humankind, not merely showy words that mean little and help not at all.

Mark Hamilton

Why Have You Forsaken Me?

Psalm 22:1-26

Mark Shipp & Jerry Shipp

Mark Shipp

Why Have You Forsaken Me?

God, Have You Abandoned Me?

Adapted from Psalm 22

Randy Daw & Jeremy Daw | Randy Daw

God, Have You Abandoned Me?

Psalm 23

Translation

A psalm of David.

*1 The Lord is my shepherd; I lack nothing.

†2 He makes me recline in lush pastures; he leads me beside placid waters.

*3 He restores my life; he conducts me along straight paths for the sake of his name.

†4 Also, when I go in the valley of gloom, I will fear no evil, for you are with me. Your rod
and staff console me.

†5 You spread out a table for me in front of my enemies. You anoint my head with oil;
my cup[a] overflows.

*6 Surely good and steadfast love will pursue me all the days of my life, and I will dwell[b]
in the Lord's house for a long time.[c]

[a] The Septuagint reads "your cup" instead of "my cup," emphasizing the role of God as host of the banquet and owner of all the dishes on the table. While the Septuagint reading seems more likely to be original, the weight of English translations and their usage in the church's worship leads us to follow the Hebrew MT in this case. Probably "your cup" is the better reading, though the image differs little in implication.

[b] Several ancient versions correct the Hebrew "and I will return . . ." to "and I will dwell . . ."

[c] Literally "length of days."

Structure and Poetry

This famous gem of a psalm expresses trust in God. It revolves around two related images: care of sheep (vv. 1–4) and hospitality at a banquet (vv. 5–6). Both images bespeak the generosity and tenderness, yet dependability, of God.

Verse 1's image of the shepherd is common in the Bible and the ancient Near East. An interesting companion text might be Isaiah 40:11, which speaks of the shepherd who can protect and guide the flock, but does so with exquisite tenderness, allowing for every possible reaction to the shepherd on the sheep's part. In verse 2, the image is self-explanatory, but since luxurious pastures are comparatively rare in some parts of the land of Israel, the emotional intensity of the verse should not be missed. Finding God is finding comfort and relief. Verse 3 makes this idea even clearer. The "straight paths" at one level are the smooth trails shepherds hope to take sheep along, but the metaphor refers ultimately to the moral and spiritual guidance God offers. Verse 4 refers to the deep ravines of the land of Israel, which often have sections that are in perpetual shadow because the cliffs are so close together. Such places are inherently dangerous and frightening (rockslides, lurking predators). Even there, however, the shepherd can protect the flock. Since the psalm uses shepherding metaphors to refer to everyday life, the verse must refer to passages in life that seem to lack hope altogether.

The image of shepherd also applies in ancient Near Eastern texts to kings and even deities. Thus Israel's God "shepherds" the people by rescuing them from their enemies (Ps. 80:1), and they in return consider themselves a saved flock (Pss. 79:13; 95:7; 100:3; Isa. 40:10–11). Perhaps the kingly imagery is also in play in Psalm 23, though it may also be the case that Israelite poets thought of salvation, kingship, and shepherding as terms that could relate, but need not always do so.

In verse 5, the metaphor shifts to hospitality, and we see God as the gracious host who gives guests more than they can possibly want. Anointing with oil, a sign of welcome, has the practical benefit of bringing some level of comfort. The banquet is lavish. Most surprisingly, it occurs before one's enemies, indicating that the humiliation that the righteous sometimes face because of their stand for the true and the good will come to an end.

In verse 6, the psalmist hopes to live in the temple itself, where he or she can pray and share in the sacrifices and thus the life of the Spirit as long as life lasts. The temple thus becomes a visible sign of God's protection of Israel.

Theology and Application

This tiny psalm has been immensely popular, perhaps because it states in a few verses the beauty of trust in God. Psalm 23 expresses the utter dependence of the faithful person on God. The sheep merely follows and eats, and the guest merely enjoys the banquet. God does all the important work, and we respond with gratitude.

At the same time, the psalmist is not naive. He or she expects trouble, has enemies, and seeks refuge from the everyday mess of the world. Biblical faith does not embrace fantasy, but offers the quiet hope that God is at work every moment, enabling those who believe to survive and flourish.

The temple is important in this psalm (see Ps. 84 for the deep emotional resonance that the temple had for ancient Israelites). It symbolized God's real presence among the people. It was a constant reminder of the mighty deeds of salvation in the past. In the post-exilic period, it also reminded everyone that God could discipline the people, and had done so. The temple is not a talisman, but it is a holy place in the highest sense of the word.

For Those Who Sing Psalm 23

We trust God because we have found God to be interested in our well-being and to demonstrate this interest over a long time. This interest shows up in practical ways, symbolized by the provision of food in this text, and it also manifests itself in the almost wasteful generosity of God. Divine extravagance creates an environment of graciousness and comfort for human beings, which we experience most fully when in the presence of God, whether in Israel's temple or the gathering of the church.

Mark Hamilton

The Lord My Shepherd Is

Psalm 23

Kathleen Kirkland-Kanewske

Kathleen Kirkland-Kanewske

The Lord Is My Shepherd

(I Lie Down in Pastures Green)

Mark Shipp & Michael E. Showalter — *Psalm 23* — Michael E. Showalter

The Lord Is My Shepherd

The Lord Is My Shepherd

Psalm 23

Konstantin Zhigulin
Trans. Mark Shipp

Konstantin Zhigulin

Psalm 24

Translation

Of David. A psalm.

*1 The earth belongs to the LORD and its fullness, the world and those who dwell in it.
*2 For on the seas *he*[a] founded it, and on the rivers he established it.

†3 Who shall go up to the hill of the LORD? And who shall stand in his holy place?
*4 *He who*[b] is clean of hands and pure of heart, who does not lift up his soul to what is false and does not swear deceitfully.
*5 He will receive blessing from the LORD and righteousness from the God of his salvation.
*6 This is the generation of those who seek him, who seek the face of the God of Jacob.[c]

†7 Lift up your heads, O gates! Yea, be lifted up, O everlasting doors! And[d] the king of glory will[e] come in.
†8 Who is this king of glory?
*The LORD strong and mighty, the LORD mighty of[f] battle.
†9 Lift up your heads, O gates! Yea, be lifted up, O everlasting doors! And[d] the king of glory will[e] come in.
†10 Who is this king of glory?
*The LORD of Hosts, he is the king of glory.

[a] There is a strong emphasis on *he* (Yahweh) in the first line.

[b] These words are not in the Hebrew, but the context requires their insertion in order to make sense of this verse.

[c] The translation of the second half of verse 6 here follows the Septuagint and Syriac. "The God of Jacob" is an appropriate parallel to "him" in the first half. The Hebrew has "who seeks your face, O Jacob," which does not make sense in this context.

[d] Or "that."

[e] Or "may."

[f] Or "in."

Structure and Poetry

Verses 1–2: Worshipers declare their faith that the LORD owns the whole earth and the people who inhabit it.

Verses 3–6: Worshipers ask the officiating priest about the type of person who may enter the LORD's temple and worship him (v. 3), and the priest states three characteristics the LORD seeks: clean hands, a pure heart, and genuineness (vv. 4–6). The same pattern appears in Psalm 15. Scholars label poetic pieces like this "Entrance Liturgies."

Verses 7–10: This liturgy occurs as the procession of worshipers approaches the gates of the temple.

Theology and Application

Worshipers are entering the presence of the owner of the whole earth. Those who approach the sanctuary to worship the LORD must love the LORD with their whole heart and love their neighbors as themselves. By "going up" to the hill of the LORD (which is the Jerusalem temple in this context), they are voluntarily placing themselves under the rule of the king who lives there, that is, the LORD.

"Soul" in verse 4 is not "the eternal part of a human being," but rather "life," or "breath of life" (compare with Gen. 2:7). The idea that the soul is eternal comes from Greek philosophy, not from the Bible. "What is false" refers to "false gods" or "idols" (see Ps. 31:7; Jer. 18:5). "Righteousness" in verse 5 does not mean "right living," but "just judgment." God will defend the worshiper from persecutors and show him or her to be right against those who accuse falsely.

The Bible commands worshipers to "swear by God's name" that they will keep their promises (see Deut. 10:20). To "swear falsely" or "deceitfully" means that a person promises to do something but fails to keep what is promised. The God into whose presence these worshipers come is "the king of glory," who leads his angelic and human "hosts" into battle and defeats his enemies because of his superior "strength" (see Pss. 93:1; 96:6–7; 99:4). This portrayal of the LORD as a mighty warrior appears also in Exodus 15:1–10.

It is inappropriate and unbecoming to presume to worship the LORD nonchalantly or without proper preparation of heart and life. All creation silently declares Yahweh's "glory" (splendor, magnificence) daily by doing what the LORD created it to do (see Ps. 19:1–4). "Clean hands" and "pure hearts" are the essence of godly character (see James 4:8). "Clean hands" suggests the worshiper had striven to treat his fellow human beings with dignity and love. "Pure heart" suggests the worshiper's motives are God-centered and have no hidden agendas (see Ps. 73:1).

For Those Who Sing Psalm 24

As faithful followers of God approach their "king of glory," they naturally extol God as the owner and sustainer of the whole world and all who live on planet earth. They also naturally desire to approach God appropriately with clean hands, a pure heart, and genuineness or authenticity. Hypocrisy abounds in public worship services; thus, true worshippers desire to be and behave entirely differently.

John Willis

The Lord Our God Created Earth

Psalm 24

Jennifer Hall

Mel Witcher

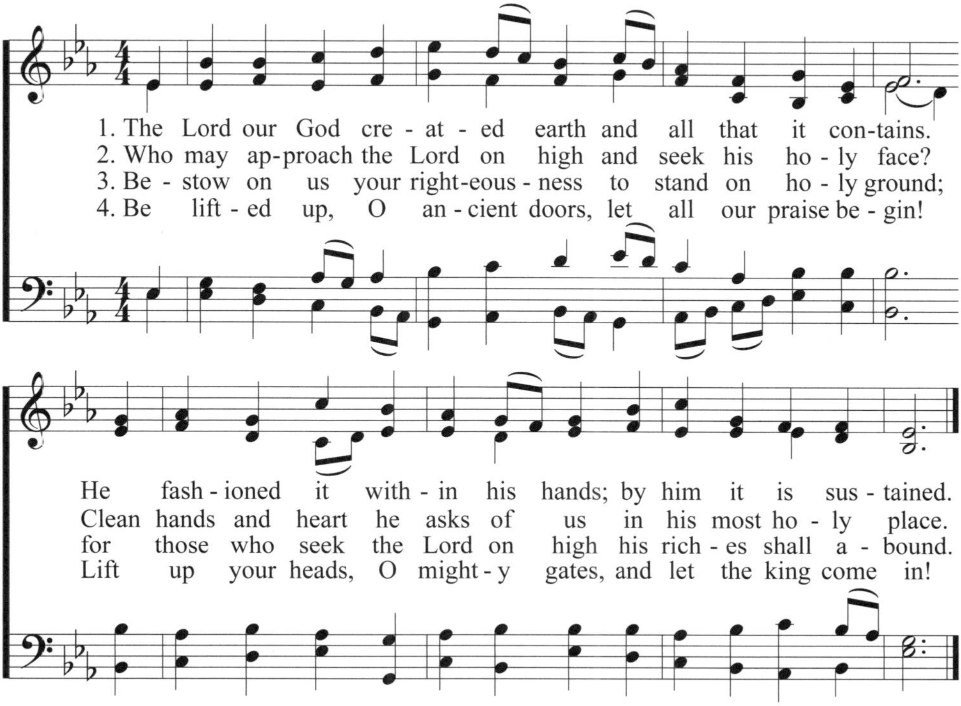

Who Is the King of Glory?

Adapted from Psalm 24

Ashley Gay | Kathy Thompson

Who Is the King of Glory?

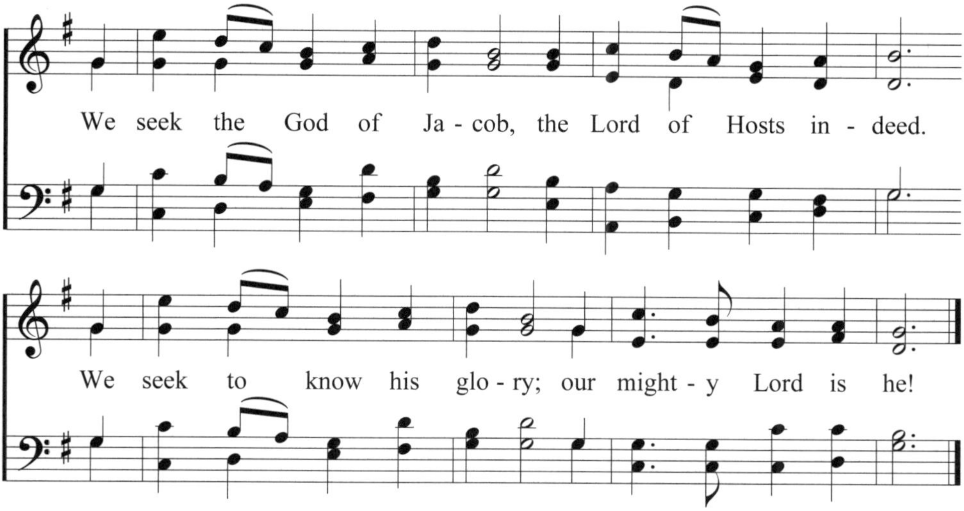

Who Shall Ascend?

Psalm 24:3-5

From the oratorio *Hinds' Feet on High Places*

Mark Shipp & Jerry Shipp

Rachel McInturff
Arr. Randy Daw & Rachel McInturff

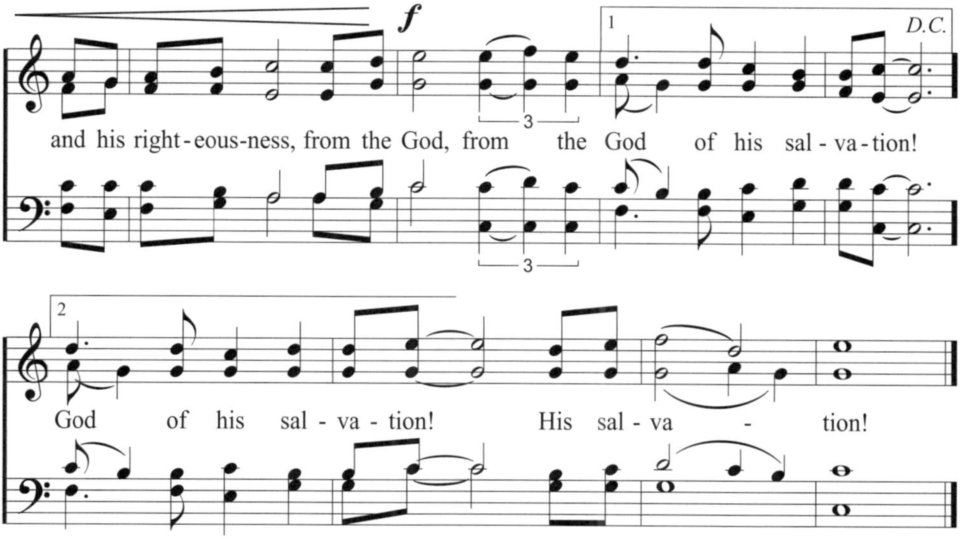
f
1
D.C.
and his right-eous-ness, from the God, from the God of his sal-va-tion!
3
3
2
God of his sal-va-tion! His sal-va-tion!

PSALM 25

Translation

Of David.

†1 (א, *aleph*) Unto you, O LORD, my soul I lift up.

†2 (ב, *bet*) O my God, in you I trust; do not let me be shamed; do not let my enemies rejoice over me.

†3 (ג, *gimel*) Also, all those who wait for you, let them not be shamed; let those who betray others' confidence maliciously be shamed.

*4 (ד, *dalet*) Your ways, O LORD, cause me to know; your paths, teach me.

*5 (ה, *he*, and ו, *waw*) Lead me in your faithfulness[a] and teach me, for you are the God of my salvation; for you I wait all the day.

†6 (ז, *zayin*) Remember your mercy, O LORD, and your steadfast love, for they are from eternity.

*7 (ח, *het*) Do not remember the sins of my youth and my transgressions; according to your steadfast love remember me for the sake of your goodness, O LORD.

†8 (ט, *tet*) Good and upright is the LORD; therefore, he teaches sinners in the way.

†9 (י, *yod*) He leads humble people in justice, and teaches humble people his way.

*10 (כ, *kaph*) All the paths of the LORD are steadfast love and faithfulness for those who keep his covenant and his decrees.

*11 (ל, *lamed*) For the sake of your name, O LORD, forgive my iniquity, for it is great.

†12 (מ, *mem*) Who is the person who reveres the LORD? He will instruct him in the way he will choose.

†13 (נ, *nun*) His soul in goodness will lodge, and his descendants will inherit the land.

*14 (ס, *samek*) The secret[b] of the LORD is for the ones revering him, and to cause them to know[c] his covenant.

†15 (ע, *ayin*) My eyes are continually toward the LORD, for he will bring my feet out of the net.

†16 (פ, *pe*) Turn to me and be gracious to me, for lonely and afflicted am I.

*17 (צ, *tsade*) The troubles of my heart are enlarged; from my distresses bring me out.

*18 (ר, *resh*) Consider my affliction and my trouble, and forgive all my sins.

†19 (ר, *resh*)[d] Consider my enemies, for they are many, and the violent hatred[e] with which they hate me.

*20 (ש, *shin*) Guard my soul[f] and deliver me; do not let me be shamed, for I take refuge in you.
*21 (ת, *taw*) May integrity and uprightness preserve me, for I wait for you.
*22 Redeem Israel, O God, from all her troubles.

[a] Or "truth." The Hebrew word *'emet* appears in verses 5a and 10a and may mean "faithfulness" in both places, although several English translations render it "truth" in verse 5a.

[b] There are various ways to interpret the Hebrew word *sod* in verse 14a. The NRSV translates the word "friendship," a meaning it also assigns to this word in Job 29:4. In several texts of the Hebrew Bible, this Hebrew word means "council," "assembly," "congregation" (e.g., Pss. 89:7; 111:1; Jer. 23:18, 22), but this meaning does not fit the context of Ps. 25:14). On the basis of the use of this Hebrew word in Psalm 64:2; Proverbs 11:13; 20:19; 25:9; and Amos 3:7, as well as the context of Psalm 25:14, "secret" seems the most likely meaning here: God letting those who revere him in on his secrets (line a) is virtually the same as God causing them to know his covenant (see the same thought in Deut. 29:29, which uses a different Hebrew word for "secret things").

[c] The Hebrew is literally "he causes them to know."

[d] The *r, resh,* is repeated. There is no line for the letter *q, qoph*.

[e] The Hebrew is literally "hatred of violence."

[f] The Hebrew says *nepesh*, "soul" or "life," the self.

Structure and Poetry

Psalm 25 is an acrostic—that is, in Hebrew, each verse begins with the next letter of the Hebrew alphabet. There are three exceptions to this. First, in verse 5, the first two lines begin with the letter *h* (*he*) and the third line begins with the letter *w* (*waw*), so that two Hebrew letters appear here in the same verse. Second, the letter *q* (*qoph*) does not appear as expected in verse 18. Instead, both verses 18 and 19 begin with the letter *r* (*resh*). Finally, verse 21 begins with the final letter of the Hebrew alphabet, *t* (*taw*), so that the final verse of this psalm, verse 22, is not a part of the acrostic, formally speaking.

The audience to whom or about whom the psalmist is speaking as well as the subject matter determine the outline of Psalm 25. The pattern of this psalm is "alternating," ABABA:

A. Verses 1–7:	The psalmist addresses God directly ("you," "O Lord," "my God," etc.), pleading with him to protect him from his enemies, lead him in God's ways, and deal with him according to God's "steadfast love."
B. Verses 8–10:	The psalmist addresses an audience of fellow-believers, testifying to them that God leads the humble in the right way and deals with his people according to his "steadfast love."
A. Verse 11:	The psalmist addresses God, imploring him to forgive his sin.
B. Verses 12–15:	The psalmist addresses an audience of fellow-believers, assuring them that God is with those who "fear" [reverence, highly respect, honor] him and will teach them the way they should go.

A. Verses 16–22: The psalmist addresses God, beseeching him to forgive his sin and to protect him from his enemies.

Theology and Application

Several terms indicate that Psalm 25 is a prayer designed to teach the psalmist's community of faith God's character, the nature of humankind, and God's relationship to people. These are "cause to know" (the covenant, vv. 4, 14); "your [God's] ways" (vv. 4, 8, "the way"; v. 9, "his way"; v. 12, "the way he will choose"); "your paths" (vv. 4, 10, "the paths of the LORD"); "teach" (vv. 4, 5, 9); "your truth" (v. 5); "lead" (v. 5); "instruct" (vv. 8, 12); "justice" (v. 9); "his covenant" (vv. 10, 14); and "his decrees" (v. 10).

The expression "I lift up my soul" (to the LORD) in verse 1 recalls the same expression in 24:4b. "Lift up" is a technical term that means "to offer a sacrifice." To "lift up one's soul" means to "offer oneself to God" as a living sacrifice (see Rom. 12:1). "My soul" in 25:13 and 20 also means "the person himself." The same Hebrew word appears in the expression "lift up my sins" in 25:18, which means "forgive my sins."

Enemies bring "shame" or disgrace on their opponents (vv. 2–3, 20) by defeating them or by exposing them to public ridicule in some way. The author of Psalm 25 beseeches God to protect him from the "shame" his enemies desire to inflict on him.

God "teaches" or "leads" people who are open to his instruction by various experiences in life, failures and successes, losses and gains, victories and defeats, as well as by truths he reveals through his servants (vv. 4–5, 8). The fact that "*your* ways" and "*your* paths" appear at the beginning of verse 4 indicates this is where the psalmist puts emphasis. He desires to know God's ways and God's paths, not other ways or other paths.

To "wait" for the LORD (vv. 3, 5, and 21) apparently means to "trust" or "hope" in him, as the parallelism in Psalm 130:5–6 and the contexts in Psalm 37:9 and Isaiah 40:29–31 suggest. The psalmist implores the LORD to "remember" his mercy (v. 6a), not to "remember" the psalmist's sins and transgressions (v. 7a), and to "remember" the psalmist (v. 7b). "Remember" here means more than "call to mind." It means to act in a way appropriate to the object named. God's "name" in verse 11 means God's character. The psalmist believes that God forgives people of sins they commit and appeals to God to do so, not because of anything human beings do, but because of God's character of steadfast love, faithfulness, and goodness (vv. 7, 10, and 18).

Ancient peoples used nets made of flax, hemp, palm fiber, or papyrus as traps to capture fish, birds, and wild animals. Pillars of stone with inscriptions (called steles) dating as early as 2500 B.C.E. portray enemies of certain kings and nations caught in nets. Several texts in the Hebrew Bible refer to people trapped in nets to symbolize various types of dangers that they faced (Pss. 9:15; 10:9; 31:4; 35:7–8; 57:6; 140:5; and 141:10). The composer of Psalm 25:15 expresses the assurance that Yahweh will deliver him from dangers that his enemies place in his path.

According to God's law to Israel, one could "redeem" an animal or a person from alienation by paying a designated price (Exod. 21:8, 30; Num. 3:45–51; 18:15–16). The author of Psalm 25 uses this practice to plead with God to "redeem," that is, "deliver" Israel from all her troubles (v. 22; note the synonymous verb "deliver" in v. 20).

God uses unpleasant people and experiences as instruments to cause his people to grow and mature in trust and service. The psalmist pleads with God for help on the basis of God's mercy, grace, steadfast love, goodness, and forgiveness, which are fundamental to God's character: verses 6–7, 10–11, 16, 18 (see Exod. 34:6–7; Pss. 86:5, 15; 103:8–13.) The term "goodness" in verses 7, 8, and 13 apparently means God's goodness, which he shares with those who faithfully serve him. As often in the Bible, "to fear God" (vv. 12, 14) does not mean to be terrified by God or to be "scared to death" of God, but to stand in awe of God, to hold God in the highest respect, to "revere" God.

Teaching God's people God's ways is a vital part of the corporate worship experience: verses 4–5, 8–10, 12, 14. A servant's eyes are always focused on the master (v. 15; see Ps. 123:2), as an indication of complete trust and dependence and in order to see instruction or direction, which the master communicates by a hand signal or a facial expression. The servant does not trust her or his own initiative or judgment, but is wholly confident that her or his master knows what to do next and will communicate to the servant how that servant fits into the master's decisions and plans. In times of trouble and danger, a person may flee to God for protection, shelter, and safety as one would flee to a fortress or stronghold (v. 20).

For Those Who Sing Psalm 25

Worshippers simultaneously correspond and interact with God, fellow-worshippers, and enemies. They should sensitively and carefully express their feelings and thoughts and intentions to each personality around them. Pleas for steadfast love and forgiveness to God, assurance and encouragement to fellow-worshippers, and appeals for protection from hostile enemies are appropriate responses to complex issues and afflictions.

John Willis

My Trust I Place in God Alone

Psalm 25

Martha Pounders Walker

Randy Daw

Turn to Me, O Holy Lord

Adapted from Psalm 25

Konstantin Zhigulin
Trans. Brad Cawyer

Konstantin Zhigulin

Choral

Preserve My Soul

Psalm 25

Martha Pounders Walker

Matt Roberson

The composer's suggestions: For a choir setting, Group I should be all or most of the choir while Group II a portion of the choir. For a congregational setting, Group I should be the congregation while Group II could be a choir, praise team, or portion of the congregation.

Psalm 26

Translation

Of David.

1 Establish justice for me, O Lord, for in my complete devotion I have walked, and in the Lord I have trusted without wavering.
2 Prove me, O Lord, and try me; test my heart and my mind.
3 For your steadfast love is before my eyes, and I will walk in your faithfulness.

4 I do not sit with worthless ones, and with hypocrites I do not consort.
5 I hate the assembly of evildoers, and with wicked ones I will not sit.

6 I wash my hands in innocence, and I will go around your altar, O Lord,
7 singing aloud with a voice of thanksgiving and telling all your wondrous deeds.
8 O Lord, I love the house in which you dwell and the place where your glory abides.

9 My soul, do not gather with sinners, nor with bloodthirsty ones, my life,
10 in whose hands are evil devices, and their right hands are full of bribes.

11 But in complete devotion I walk; redeem me, and be gracious to me.
12 My foot stands on level ground; in the great assembly I will praise the Lord.

Structure and Poetry

The author of Psalm 26 approaches the Lord in prayer from beginning to end. The content of Psalm 26 suggests a chiastic, or "mirror image," structure, per the outline below:

- A. Verses 1–3: The petitioner justifies that he or she has been faithful to the Lord, summons the Lord to prove the mettle of his or her justification, and openly embraces the Lord's steadfast love and faithfulness.
- B. Verses 4–5: The petitioner sternly rejects all companionship with the wicked.
- C. Verses 6–8: The petitioner professes that his or her whole life is devoted to commitment to the temple and its every aspect.
- B'. Verses 9–10: The petitioner prays fervently that God will remove all types of wicked people who threaten his or her faithfulness to the Lord.

A′. Verses 11–12: The petitioner resolves that he or she will submit to the LORD.

Theology and Application

No true servant of God claims sinlessness, righteous achievement, or good works. The follower of God "receives" every gift and blessing from his or her Father. God's disciple completely trusts in God, lives daily by God's steadfast love and faithfulness, and receives God's redemption and grace (see vv. 1, 11; see also Pss. 89:1–2, 14, 24, 33; 117:1–2). Spiritual growth and maturity emanates from testing, endurance, and perseverance in the same way that one "proves" gold or silver in the furnace to remove alloys and refine metal (see Jer. 6:27–30; Isa. 1:22, 25; Prov. 30:5; Pss. 7:9; 17:3; 139:1–6, 23–24). The heart and life close to God rejects or flees from wicked tempters or coercive powers rather than yielding to evil forces (see vv. 4–5, 9–10). The act of "washing hands" is a symbolic expression to God and others of "washing the spiritual heart" (see v. 6; Pss. 24:4; 73:13; Jer. 4:14; James 4:8).

A vital aspect of worship is telling the assembled spiritual family "all the wondrous deeds" that the LORD declares throughout all generations from the ancient past to the very present (see v. 7; Pss. 9:1, 11; 22:22; 48:12–14; 75:1; 78:1–8; 107:22, 32; and frequent references throughout the Old and New Testaments).

The LORD's "glory" is his real, but mysterious, magnificence and splendor, constantly revealed in his presence in the heart, the temple, and the entire world (see v. 8; Pss. 8:1; 19:1; 24:7–10; 29:1–4, 9; 1 Kings 8:10–13; Ezek. 1:28; and many other references throughout Scripture). The person of prayer openly proclaims complete dependence on God. Spiritual growth and strength are possible only by passing through severe and difficult experiences. See James 1:2–4. It is great joy to dwell in the LORD's house. See verse 8.

For Those Who Sing Psalm 26

Godly people stand between God on the one hand and competing voices against God on the other. The practice of worship often consists of worshippers committing themselves to God in steadfast love and faithfulness, and at the same time resisting unspiritual, unhealthy, non-uplifting voices all around. Corporate resolution in worship puts worshippers on solid ground.

John Willis

Sing Hosanna, Praise

Psalm 26

Chris Stivers

Chris Stivers

from ev - il turn me a - way. Try me, O Lord; may my
and teach me how I should be. Help me to walk with a
heart and mind be test - ed. Lord, give me strength eve - ry day.
more com - plete de - vo - tion; re - deem and sanc - ti - fy me.
Sing ho - san - na, praise! We give thanks to you as we
shout of your won - der - ful deeds. Sing ho - san - na, praise, and we
stand with you; to - geth - er we sing hal - le - lu - jah.

Be Merciful, O God

Psalm 26

Sarah Shipp

Gary Pendergrass

Psalm 27

Translation

Of David.

*1 The LORD is my light and my salvation; whom shall I fear? The LORD is the stronghold
of my life, of whom shall I be afraid?
*2 When evildoers come near against me to devour my flesh—my adversaries and my
enemies—they shall stumble and fall.
*3 Though an army encamp against me, my heart shall not fear; though war rise up
against me, yet I will keep on trusting.
†4 One thing I asked of the LORD; I will ask it: to dwell in the house of the LORD all the
days of my life, to see the beauty of the LORD, and to inquire in his temple.
†5 For he will hide him in his shelter in the day of trouble; he will hide me in the shelter
of his tent, on a rock he will set me high.
*6 And now my head is lifted up above my enemies who are surrounding me, and I
will sacrifice in his tent sacrifices with shouts of joy; I will sing and make melody to
the LORD.

†7 Hear, O LORD, my voice; I will call; be gracious to me and answer me.
*8 To you my heart said, "Seek[a] my face." Your face, O LORD, I will seek.
*9 Do not hide your face from me; do not turn away your servant in anger. You have been
my help; do not cast me off and do not forsake me, O God of my salvation.
†10 If my father and my mother forsake me, the LORD will gather me.[b]
*11 Teach me, O LORD, your way, and lead me in a straight path because of my enemies.
†12 Do not give me up to the will[c] of my enemies, for false witnesses have arisen against
me, and they breathe out violence.

†13 I believe that I will see the goodness of the LORD in the land of the living.
*14 Wait for the LORD, be strong, and let your heart be courageous[d]; yea, wait for the LORD.

[a] "Seek" here is a plural imperative. The Septuagint says, "To you my heart said, 'He has sought my face.' Your face, O Lord, I have sought."

[b] The Septuagint says "receive me." The RSV says, "take me up."

[c] Hebrew says "soul."

[d] Hebrew says "let your heart be firm."

Structure and Poetry

Verses 1–6, 13–14:	The psalmist (perhaps a sage or musician) encourages his fellow-believers. The psalmist assures his hearers that the Lord will sustain him against his powerful enemies.
Verses 7–12:	The psalmist beseeches the Lord to protect him against his enemies, to support him, and help him endure.

Theology and Application

Even though powerful enemies and evil forces threaten those who are faithful to God, the Lord sustains his servants in all fearful circumstances (see vv. 1, 3; Pss. 3:6; 56:3–4, 11; 118:6; Heb. 13:6). The true follower of God focuses on one purpose in life: to live in the house of the Lord all the days of his life, to behold the beauty of the Lord, and to inquire in his temple (see v. 4).

The only dependable protection against sin, death, persecution, and infirmity is hiding in or being covered by the Lord's shelter (v. 5; Pss. 31:20; 32:7; 46:1–7; 61:4; 119:114; Luke 13:34). By "seeking God's face," one actually enters into and communes with God's presence. This expression does not indicate that human beings see the literal "face" of the Lord. At the same time, the Lord is actually present among his people, though unseen (see 1 Tim. 1:17; 6:16).

Experience throughout the centuries demonstrates that many times parents abandon or forsake their children. The Lord affirms that he never abandons his people (see v. 10). Servants of the Lord who have been tested persistently remind each generation to emphasize that faithful endurance is to be strong and to take courage at all times throughout life (see v. 14; Ps. 31:24; Deut. 31:7–8; Josh. 1:6–7, 9, 18; 1 Cor. 16:13–14). God is able to embolden the faithful to persevere, while facing grave fear.

Many distractions surround life, so the true disciple must seek and find the most valuable treasure of the heart (see v. 4; Matt. 13:44–46; Luke 10:38–42). God's beauty lifts us above all other attractions that life offers (v. 4). Though human aspirations or promises may fail, God is ever faithful and is a hiding place to protect and care for his servants (v. 5).

For Those Who Sing Psalm 27

In times of trouble, dangers, and sorrow, faithful followers of God desperately need encouragement, support, and consolation. The composer of Psalm 27 offers precisely this kind of support in difficult times. All true worshippers can quickly chime into the thoughts and tones of words like "be strong, and let your heart be courageous."

John Willis

One Thing I Ask

Psalm 27:4

Keith Lancaster

Keith Lancaster

Wait upon the Lord

Psalm 27

Jerry Shipp | Sean Pullen

Wait upon the Lord

Strength of My Life

Based on Psalm 27

Kathleen Kirkland-Kanewske Kathleen Kirkland-Kanewske

Psalm 28

Translation

Of David.

1 Unto you, O Lord, I call; O my Rock, do not be silent from me, lest you be silent from me and I become like ones who go down to the Pit.

2 Hear the sound of my supplications, when I cry for help to you; when I lift up my hands unto your holy place.[a]

3 Do not drag me away with wicked ones, with evildoers, who speak peace with their neighbors, but wickedness is in their heart.[b]

4 Repay[c] them according to their acts[d] and according to the evil of their deeds; according to the work of their hands, give them their recompense.

5 For they do not regard the deeds of the Lord, nor the work of his hands; he will break them down, and he will not build them up.

6 Blessed be the Lord, for he has heard the sound of my supplications.

7 The Lord is my strength and my shield; in him my heart trusts, and I am helped and my heart exults, and with[e] my song I will give thanks to him.

8 The Lord is the strength of his people, and he is the refuge of the salvation of his anointed one.

9 Save your people, and bless your inheritance; yea, be their shepherd and carry them forever.

[a] The Hebrew says "the holy of holies (the *debir*) of your holy place."

[b] In the Bible, the "heart" is not a physical organ, but the "inner" character of all life, the whole person, which at times includes the mind, the emotions, the attitude, the moods, etc. (see vv. 3, 7). Often, as in these texts, "heart" simply means "him, I, her, etc."

[c] The Hebrew says "give."

[d] The Hebrew is singular; read plural with the Septuagint.

[e] The Hebrew says "from."

Structure and Poetry

Psalm 28 is a petition or supplication to the Lord throughout. The petitioner entreats the Lord to protect and bless him (vv. 1–2, 6–7), to defeat and destroy his evil enemies (vv. 3–5), and to deliver his people (vv. 8–9). Thus, Psalm 28 has an alternating structure.

Verses 1–2: The petitioner beseeches the Lord to hear his prayer.
Verses 3–5: The petitioner implores the Lord to retaliate against evildoers.

Verses 6–7: The petitioner praises the LORD, for the LORD is a strength, shield, and help, in whom he trusts.

Verses 8–9: The petitioner is jubilant because the LORD has given his people strength and deliverance, has given his anointed king a safe refuge, has blessed his inheritance, and has led his people through secure journeys.

Theology and Application

Every human being should be realistic throughout all aspects of life. Hence, it is advisable to cry out to God in prayer to help in every situation (see vv. 1–2).

The Bible uses several metaphors to portray God's character, speech, and action. Psalm 28 describes Yahweh as a "rock" (v. 1), "strength" (vv. 7–8), "shield" (v. 7), "refuge" (v. 8), and "shepherd" (v. 9). These first four metaphors emphasize that the LORD protects those in danger or peril. The metaphor of a shepherd indicates that the LORD cares for and supplies the needs of his people. Thus, a king—the anointed one—guides his kingdom as a shepherd leads his flock (vv. 8 and 9 alternate between the figure of the anointed one and the figure of the shepherd; see for example, 2 Sam. 5:2; 7:8; and elsewhere).

God's people naturally "lift up their hands" to worship, pray, submit to, and adore the LORD in expressing corporate worship (see v. 2; Pss. 63:4; 134:2; Lam. 3:40–41; Isa. 1:15; 1 Tim. 2:8; and elsewhere). People "reap" what they "sow" (see vv. 4–5; Rom. 2:1–11; Gal. 6:7), but God's repeated reassurances and promises motivate his followers to fill their hearts with singing and thanksgiving (v. 7).

God's shepherd, and all who would imitate his example, gently beckons people like sheep, not coercing or forcing humans to do what leaders demand, but offering blessing (see v. 9; Isa. 40:11; Ezek. 34:1–16; 1 Pet. 5:1–4).

The appropriate stance of a human being is to bow down and kneel before our creator, king, and sustainer (see Ps. 95:6). It is easy to say that one is true to his creator or to flatter a trusted friend, but such a person soon reveals that his heart is hypocritical and self-centered (see v. 3; Jer. 12:2; Titus 1:16). Many find "security" in various promises. God alone is a dependable refuge (vv. 7–8; see Pss. 7:1; 18:2; 46:1–7; 118:8–9).

For Those Who Sing Psalm 28

Metaphors are powerful instruments of speech in sermons, prayers, and songs. The composer of Psalm 28 artfully combines the metaphors of "rock," "strength," "shield," "refuge," and "shepherd," attempting to portray God as the object of worship. Worshippers should carefully ponder the meaning and significance of each metaphor. There is no way to comprehend God fully, but metaphors are very helpful.

John Willis

I Cry Out to You

Psalm 28

Laura K. Collum

Ruth Ann Somervell

In Your Refuge

Psalm 28

Rachel Shipp

Ruth Ann Somervell

PSALM 29

Translation

A Song. Of David.

1 Attribute to the LORD, O heavenly beings,[a] attribute to the LORD glory and power;
2 Attribute to the LORD the glory due his name. Worship the LORD in all his holy splendor.

3 The voice of the LORD is over the waters: the God of glory thunders; the LORD thunders
over the mighty waters.
4 The voice of the LORD is powerful; the voice of the LORD is majestic.
5 The voice of the LORD shatters the cedars; the LORD shatters the cedars of Lebanon.
6 He makes Lebanon prance like a calf and Hermon[b] like a young wild ox.
7 The voice of the LORD ignites flashes of lightning.
8 The voice of the LORD rocks the wilderness. The LORD rocks the wilderness of Qadesh.
9 The voice of the LORD causes the oaks to sway[c] and strips the forest bare. Meanwhile—
in his temple—all are saying, "Glory!"

10 The LORD sits enthroned over the flood; the LORD sits as king forever.
11 The LORD protects his people; the LORD blesses his people with peace.

[a] "O heavenly beings" also appears in the NRSV, while the NIV reads, "O mighty ones." The Hebrew literally reads, "sons of God."

[b] "Hermon." The Hebrew reads "Syrion," which is another name for Mount Hermon, a 9,200 foot peak on the border of modern-day Syria and Lebanon.

[c] "Causes the oaks to sway." This can also be read, "causes the deer to give birth."

Structure and Poetry

Structurally, the psalm is easily divided into three parts:

Part One (vv. 1–2) is a call to worship.

The "heavenly beings" thus summoned are elsewhere called "heavenly host," "angels/messengers," or "council of the holy ones." They are not lesser gods but God's heavenly attendants.

Part Two (vv. 3–9) gives the reason to praise God: his powerful, irresistible "voice."

Even the strongest, most enduring elements of the natural world—the great sea, the strongest trees, the tallest mountains, the most desolate wilderness—are subject to God's commands.

God's "voice" booms out like thunder (v. 3)—the loudest sound heard in the ancient world. God's voice likewise sets off great flashes of lightning (v. 7), which can be both brilliant to see and terrible to feel (when they strike the ground, or ignite fires).

The movement of God's "voice" is from west to east: from the "mighty waters" (the Mediterranean Sea) inland to the mountains of Lebanon and on to the wilderness areas to the east and south.

No wonder, then, that already in God's "temple" his worshippers have assembled to shout "glory!" to his name (v. 9c).

Part Three (vv. 10–11) is a final affirmation of God's enduring reign and protection of his people.

After the tumult of verses 3–9 comes the unexpected quietness, the tranquility of verses 10–11. This is the final result of God's eternal rule (v. 10): a "blessed assurance" to his people of his care and protection. It is not without irony that, after all the thunder and lightning, the shattering and quaking, the final word of the psalm is *shalom*—"peace."

Psalm 29 is often identified as one of the oldest psalms in the Psalter. The psalm resembles ancient Canaanite poetry that honors Ba'al, who is regularly identified with thunder and lightning. More important, Psalm 29 is similar to the oldest Hebrew poetry that we have—the victory songs of Moses (Exod. 15:1–12) and of Deborah (Judg. 5:4–5).

Three words in the psalm stand out. The first is *Yahweh*, the personal name of God (rendered "the LORD" in the NIV and NRSV). The name appears eighteen times in eleven verses. Make no mistake: it is "Yahweh God" who rules the world—"Yahweh God," and none other.

The second word is *voice*—the *voice* of God—which appears seven times in verses 3–9. God's control over the world is exercised through the "sound" of his "voice," just as "in the beginning" (Gen. 1:3, 6, 9, etc.).

The third word is *glory*. The glorification of God (vv. 1, 2, 3, 9) is the goal of the psalm. The Hebrew word for "glory" literally means "heaviness, abundance," and, by extension, "splendor, majesty, magnificence." Both those on earth (v. 9) and those in heaven (v. 1) are summoned to give God the glory that he so richly deserves.

Theology and Application

Psalm 29 has at least three theological words to say to us, the first of which is "power." We sometimes shy away from the notion of "power," assuming that power is inherently bad or evil. Not so in the Bible. It is not a question of "should power be used in this world?" Instead, the question is, who has the power and how should it be used? The answer to the question of "who has the power?" is, of course, God, who consistently demonstrates how he uses power to accomplish his good goals. From the creation of the world to its final consummation, from the splitting of the Sea for Israel to pass through to the resurrection of Jesus from the dead, from the provision of manna in the wilderness to Jesus' healing the lame and the blind—as Adelaide Pollard wrote, "power, all power, surely is thine."

The second theological word of Psalm 29 for us today is the word "peace." The security, the wholeness that *shalom* connotes is still needed. In keeping with the constant witness of Scripture—from "The LORD bless you and keep you . . . and give you peace" (Num. 6:24–26) to "Peace I leave with you; my peace I give to you" (John 14:27)—Psalm 29 reminds us that our goal is God's goal as well.

The third theological word of Psalm 29 that captures our attention is the word "glory." It is a word that should lead us straight to worship. To acknowledge the awesome majesty of God—to name God and God alone as the final source of power and goodness—will not only give God the praise due him but will also satisfy our hunger and need for worship.

For Those Who Sing Psalm 29

Power is a necessary, even vital component of the world in which we live. When the power goes out, the lights go off. When I am powerless, I am vulnerable and afraid. But power can be abused and misused, resulting in great harm. Psalm 29 speaks of power and makes three daring, wonderful claims: first, Jehovah God is powerful—more powerful than anyone or anything else in all creation. Second, God always uses his great power for good, to bring about peace for his people. Third, the only response to such a good and powerful God is to give him glory: "attribute to the LORD the glory due his name" (v. 2).

Paul Watson

Ascribe to the Lord

Psalm 29

Jeff Matteson

Jeff Matteson
Arr. by Konstantin Zhigulin

mp
Crescendo
And all in his tem-ple cry:"Glo - ry, glo - ry, wor-ship the Lord in
And all in his tem-ple cry:"Glo - ry, wor - ship in
mf
ho-ly ar-ray." A - scribe to the Lord the hon-or that's due him and
ho-ly ar-ray." A - scribe to the Lord the hon-or that's due him, and
1, 2, 3
4
wor-ship the Lord in ho-ly ar-ray. ho-ly ar-ray.
wor-ship the Lord in ho - ly, ho-ly ar-ray. ho-ly ar-ray.

The Voice of Jehovah

Psalm 29

Glover Shipp

Ruth Ann Somervell

Psalm 30

Translation

A psalm. A song for the dedication of the temple.[a] Of David.

†1 I will exalt you, O Lord, for you lifted me up and did not allow my enemies to gloat over me.

†2 O Lord, my God, I cried to you for help, and you made me well again.

†3 O Lord, you brought my soul up from *Sheol*;[b] you exempted me from those going down to the Pit.

*4 Sing praises to the Lord, you who are faithful to him; give thanks for the memory of his holiness.

*5 For his anger lasts only a moment, while his favor lasts for a lifetime. Weeping may last all night long, but in the morning comes a shout of joy.

†6 Now in my prosperity I would say, "Never will I be shaken—never."

†7 O Lord, it was by your favor that you had made me like a fortified peak.[c] But when you turned your face away from me, I shook like a leaf.

*8 Unto you, O Lord, I cried out; unto my Lord I pled for mercy.

†9 What profit is there in my destruction,[d] my going down to the Pit? Will the dust sing your praises? Will it declare your faithfulness?

*10 Hear, O Lord, and be merciful to me. O Lord, be my helper.

*11 You turned my ritual mourning into joyful dancing; you removed my mourning clothes and refitted me with joy,

*12 so that I might sing your praise from the bottom of my heart and never be silent.

*O Lord, my God, to you forever will I give thanks.

[a] "Temple." This could also be translated "palace." The Hebrew literally reads "house of David."

[b] "*Sheol*." The realm of the dead; see Psalm 6:5. "The Pit" is a synonym; see Psalm 28:1.

[c] "Fortified peak." NIV and NRSV both read "mountain." Fortified cities or garrisons were regularly built on mountain tops.

[d] "My destruction." This could also be read, "my silence." See NIV footnote, "if I am silenced," and verse 12, "and never be silent."

Structure and Poetry

Psalm 30 is a typical individual psalm of thanksgiving: note the occurrence of the verb "to give thanks" in verses 4, 9, and 12 (the very last word of the psalm in the Hebrew text).

The psalm begins with a focus on God and how God has saved the psalmist's life (vv. 1–3; note the three-fold invocation of God: "O Lord").

This declaration of God's deliverance is followed by an invitation to others to join in praising God (v. 4), an invitation based on the psalmist's own experience of God's enduring favor (v. 5).

Verses 6–12a are a retrospect of the psalmist's relationship with God. At first it was all about "me" for the psalmist (v. 6). Quickly, however, the psalmist realized that God was in control of his life at all times (v. 7). That realization led to a fervent plea to God for help (vv. 8–10), which God answered (v. 11), enabling the psalmist to live a new life of praise (v. 12a). The psalm closes (v. 12b) with a pledge of eternal gratitude, freely and joyfully expressed.

Not to be missed is the complex pattern of alternations that occur throughout the psalm:

Verse 1: "I will exalt (literally, 'raise you up') . . . you lifted me (literally, 'drew me out')."
Verse 3: "You brought me up . . . did not let me go down."
Verse 5a: God's short-lived anger, long-lived favor.
Verse 5b: A night-time of weeping gives way to a shout of joy at daybreak.
Verse 7: When God looked my way . . . when God turned away.
Verse 11: Wailing gives way to dancing, sackcloth is replaced by new clothes.
Verse 12a: Song, not silence, will predominate in the psalmist's new life.

Theology and Application

As are all the psalms, Psalm 30 is intensely personal. Nevertheless, the focus of the psalm is not on the person, but on God. The psalmist does not attribute his recovery from some deadly illness to luck or good fortune, nor to his own righteousness (as if he "deserved" to live). His recovery is due solely to God's favor (v. 5) and to God's actions. Note the five verbs in verses 1–3: "lifted me up," "did not allow my enemies to gloat over me," "made me well," "brought my soul up", "exempted me" from death. All five have *God* as the subject, the one who acted on behalf of the sufferer. Then again at the end of the psalm, it is God who has turned mourning to dancing and has exchanged funeral garb for new clothes. Thus, first and last, it is God who has intervened on behalf of the worshipper, who now realizes that without such divine intervention, his life would have been lost.

All this is accentuated in verses 6–7, the "hinge" of the psalm. Here the psalmist admits his former, misplaced self-confidence, and his taking God for granted—a temptation as old as Israel (Deut. 8:17–18), as current as today. Thus, the psalmist both confesses his own inability to sustain himself and praises God for giving him new life.

Some readers are troubled by the rhetorical questions of verse 9, questions that may sound like bribery. However, they may also be taken as the psalmist's deep desire to live, no longer for himself, but in order to praise God. The psalmist seeks a new vocation in life, one that is not dedicated to self-congratulation (as in v. 6), but to praising God. Having prayed to God to spare his life (v. 8), he now lives to praise God "forever" (v. 12).

Finally, it is worth noting that as personal as this psalm is, it is not private. Fellow worshippers of God—then and now—are invited in verse 4 to join in this song of praise.

For Those Who Sing Psalm 30

One of our most persistent self-delusions is that of personal independence—the notion that we are self-made men and women. Occasionally we acknowledge the secondary help that we receive from God, but *we* are still primary, for after all, "the Lord helps those who help themselves." Through hard experience, this psalmist had learned a deeper, truer lesson: our well-being, our very lives, depend not on ourselves, but on God. Once upon a time, says the psalmist, "in my prosperity I would say, 'Never will I be shaken—never'" (v. 6). But now he knew that it was by God's favor that he lived or died (v. 7). God's sustaining will is cause for deep rejoicing and for praise: "You turned my ritual mourning into joyful dancing . . . . O LORD, my God, to you forever will I give thanks" (vv. 11–12).

Paul Watson

Shout of Joy

Psalm 30

Jerry Shipp

Randy Daw

garb to robes a - new. O Lord, my God, to you will I give
praise and from my heart a shout of joy will raise! A
1, 2, 3
shout of joy will raise.
4
shout of joy will raise!

Joy in the Morning

Psalm 30

Marva L. Hughes

Marva L. Hughes

PSALM 31

Translation

For the director. A psalm of David.

1 In you, O LORD, I seek refuge. Let me never be made ashamed; by your righteousness,
deliver me.
2 Turn your ear toward me. Rescue me—quickly. Be my rock, my fortress, my strong-
hold—deliver me.
3 For you are indeed my rock, my stronghold; lead me, guide me—for your name's sake.
4 Free me from the net they have secretly set for me, for you are my fortress.
5 I am putting my life into your hands; redeem me, O LORD, faithful God.

6 I detest[a] those who rely on worthless idols, for I trust in the LORD.
7 I will shout with joy, I will rejoice in your steadfast love, because you have seen my afflic-
tion; you have observed my soul's distress.
8 And you have not handed me over to my enemy; instead, you have set my feet in a
wide-open place.

9 Have mercy on me, O LORD, for I am in distress. My eyes have become weak with
anguish, my soul and body as well.
10 For my life has been filled with troubles; my years, with groaning. My strength fails
because of my transgression,[b] and my bones waste away.
11 To all my adversaries I have become an object of scorn—even more so to my neighbors;
a source of dread to those who know me. Those who see me on the street avoid me.
12 I have been forgotten, like the dead. I have become like a broken utensil.
13 For I hear the rumors of many—horror all around! They plot against me; they conspire
to take my life.

14 But I trust in you, O LORD; I confess, "You are my God."
15 My life is in your hands; deliver me from the hand of my enemies, my pursuers.
16 Let your face shine upon your servant; save me by your steadfast love.
17 O LORD, do not put me to shame, for I am calling on you. Instead, let the wicked be put
to shame; let them be silent in *Sheol*.
18 Silence their lying lips; they speak haughtily, contemptuously against the righteous.

19 How great is your goodness that you have reserved for those who fear you, that you
perform for those who take refuge in you—in full view of everyone.
20 With the refuge of your presence you protect them from the conspiracies of men; in
your shelter you safeguard them from false accusations.

21 Blessed be the Lord, for he has marvelously shown his steadfast love to me when I was
like a city under siege.
22 In my alarm I said, "I have been cut off[c] from your sight." But you heard my cry—"Save
me!"—when I called to you for help.
23 Love the Lord, all you faithful. The Lord preserves those who are true to him, but he
repays in full those who act arrogantly.
24 So be strong, and take heart, all you who wait for the Lord.

[a] "I detest." The NIV and the Hebrew text agree ("I hate"). The NRSV reads, "you hate," along with the Greek and the Syriac. "I hate" fits better with verses 5 ("I am putting my life") and 7 ("I will shout with joy").

[b] "My transgression." So the Hebrew text ("guilt"). NIV has "affliction " and NRSV has "misery."

[c] "I have been cut off." NRSV reads, "I am driven far."

Structure and Poetry

Psalm 31 has all the features of an individual lament—a plea to God for help; a description of personal threats and challenges; a declaration of trust in God; an invitation for others to join in praising God—but not in any clear order or logical progression. One way to outline the psalm is as follows:

Verses 1–5:	Plea for help and statement of trust.
Verses 6–8:	Anticipated response to God's deliverance.
Verses 9–13:	Extended description of the psalmist's predicament.
Verses 14–18:	Plea for help and statement of trust (echoing vv. 1–5).
Verses 19–20:	Generalized praise for God's deliverance (echoing vv. 6–8).
Verses 21–22:	Psalmist's predicament and cry for help (echoing vv. 9–13).
Verses 23–24:	Summons to love God and to wait for him.

Notice that the psalm literally begins and ends with God (and not with the psalmist, nor with the psalmist's enemies, nor with the faithful): "In you, O Lord, I seek refuge" (v. 1), and "all you who wait for the Lord" (v. 24).

The prevailing attitude of the psalmist is that of confidence in God: "I *trust* in the Lord" (vv. 6, 14); "In you, O Lord, I *seek refuge*" (v. 1; cf. vv. 19b, 20a).

God is the worshipper's "rock," "fortress," "stronghold," and "shelter" (vv. 2, 3, 20).

The two most memorable expressions in the psalm appear in verses 5 and 15 respectively: "I am putting my life into your hands" (or, as the NIV translates it, "Into your hands I commit my spirit") and "My life is in your hands" (or, "my times are in your hands").

Theology and Application

The author of Psalm 31 has experienced dreadful, prolonged suffering, both physical and spiritual: "my life has been filled with troubles; my years, with groaning" (vv. 9–10). That suffering has been intensified by the scorn heaped upon him by his enemies (vv. 4, 11a, 13). Even his friends and neighbors have forgotten him (v. 11b), or avoided him (v. 12). And, assuming verse 10b is correctly translated, the psalmist's own sins have contributed to his misery. As bleak and forlorn as this self-description might be, many today will resonate with it, in part if not in whole. As someone has put it, "Life is hard; and then you die."

But that is not the whole picture, not the whole story—not for this one who has turned his life completely over to God. Greater than his own personal agony and inadequacy is the "steadfast love" of God (vv. 7, 16, 21). In his own weakness, he has sought God's strength, and God has not let him down (vv. 2–3, 19–20). This psalm thus reminds us that God loves us, blesses us, and protects us, not only when we are upright and pure, but even when we are weak and sinful, provided we commit ourselves totally to God: "I am putting my life into your hands" (v. 5).

Those were the words of Christ himself as he died on the cross (Luke 23:46), the words on Stephen's lips as he was being stoned (Acts 7:59). Many "faithful ones" (v. 23)—from Polycarp, Jerome, and Bernard of Clairvaux to Martin Luther and John Knox—have similarly departed this life repeating those words. Nevertheless, in the context of the psalm, they are the words of a person who turns over his or her entire life to God: "I am putting my life into your hands (v. 5) . . . I trust in you, O LORD (v. 14) . . . My life is in your hands (v. 15)."

This is a person, we might add, who invites us to commit ourselves to God as he has done: to "love" God (see Deut. 6:4–5); to be "faithful" and "true" to God; to "be strong" and "take heart," and to "wait for the LORD" (vv. 23–24). That is the final, evangelistic summons of Psalm 31.

For Those Who Sing Psalm 31

When the chips are down—when your future, your very life is on the line—whom do you trust? Your family? A close friend? The doctor? Your minister or spiritual advisor? As well-meaning and as capable as any of those may be, for our psalmist there was only one answer: "I trust in the LORD" (v. 6). In the face of intense and prolonged suffering (vv. 9–10) and rejection by friends and foes alike (vv. 11–13), we, too, may say, "I trust in you, O LORD" (v. 14), "my life is in your hands" (v. 15), and "I am putting my life into your hands" (v. 5). So prayed and confessed this psalmist. So said the Christ (Luke 23:46). So may we learn to say for ourselves today.

Paul Watson

In You, O Lord, Do I Take Refuge

Psalm 31

Linda Gregersen

Debbie Dorman

My Life Is in Your Hands

Sarum Graduale
Psalm 31

Linda Gregersen

Music from Sarum Graduale, 1527
Adapted by Jack Boyd

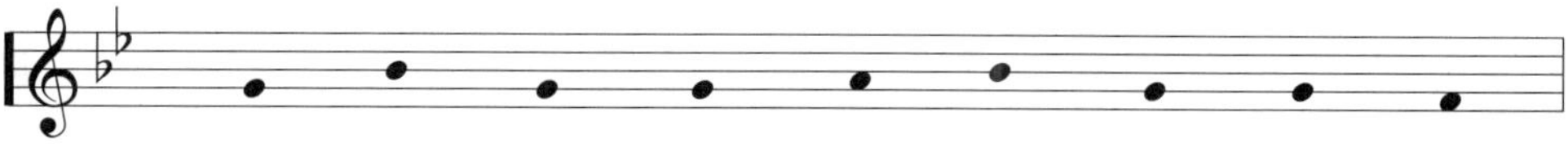

1. In you, O Lord, do I seek ref - uge!
2. The en - e - my seeks to de - stroy me—
3. De - liv - er me from those who shame me;
4. My friends, who once were true and faith - ful,
5. I have be - come a bro - ken ves - sel
6. I bless your ho - ly name for - ev - er;

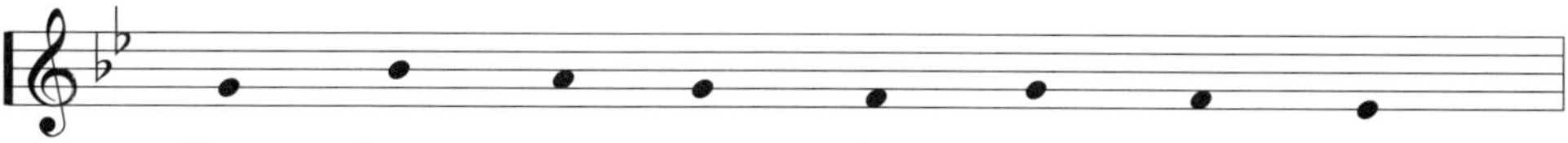

Come hear my cry; fly to my side.
I groan in an - guish and in grief!
my life is in your lov - ing hands.
for - get me as if I were dead.
as ter - ror haunts me, night and day.
your faith - ful love to me is shown.

My rock, my strong - hold, and my for - tress,
My bod - y fails, my strength grows wea - ry;
Your good - ness will sus - tain me ev - er;
My en - e - mies con - spire a - gainst me—
Con - tempt and scorn are with me ev - er.
Be strong, take heart, all who are wea - ry;

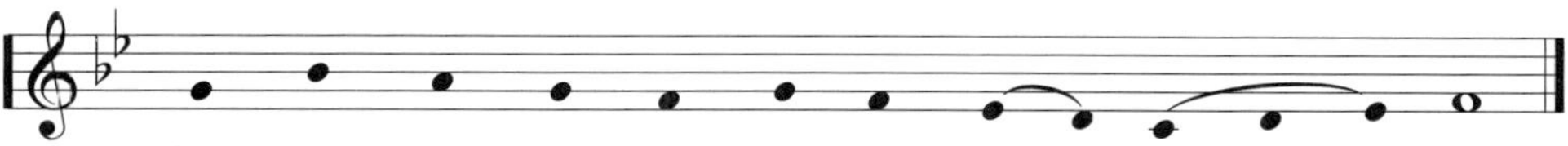

for your name's sake, Lord, be my guide. A - men.
I cry to you for my re - lief. A - men.
in you a - lone I take my stand. A - men.
they fill me with a name-less dread. A - men.
Oh, who will take my pain a - way? A - men.
take heart and hope in God a - lone. A - men.

My Life Is Filled with Deep Distress

Psalm 31

Linda Gregersen

Debbie Dorman

Psalm 32

Translation

Of David. A maskil.[a]

*1 Blessed is the one whose sin has been taken away, whose transgression has been covered.
†2 Blessed is the one to whom the Lord attaches no guilt, the one in whose spirit there is no deceit.

*3 While I remained silent, my body was exhausted from my groaning all day long,
*4 for day and night your hand lay heavy upon me; my tongue shriveled up[b] as if by summer drought.

*5 Then I acknowledged my transgression to you; my guilt I no longer covered up. I said, "I will confess my sin to the Lord," and you took away my guilt and my transgression.

*6 Therefore, let everyone who is faithful praise you; in times of distress[c] the floodwaters shall not reach him.
*7 You are my hiding place. You protect me from harm; you surround me with shouts of deliverance.
†8 Now let me teach you, show you the path to take; let me advise you, for I have my eye on you.
†9 Don't be stubborn like a horse or mule whose attention must be restrained by bridle and bit, or else it will not stay near you.
†10 The wicked have many woes; but the one who trusts in the Lord—steadfast love surrounds him!

*11 Rejoice in the Lord and shout with joy, oh righteous ones; sing out, all you who are upright in heart.

[a] *Maskil* is possibly a "wisdom" or "cult" song, but its exact meaning is unclear.

[b] "Shriveled up." The NIV reads "sapped;" the NRSV reads "dried up."

[c] "In times of distress." The Hebrew—"at a time of finding only"—is unclear. The NRSV reads, "at a time of distress." The NIV reads, "while you may be found."

Structure and Poetry

Compared to Psalm 31, the thought progression of Psalm 32 is quite clear.

Verses 1–2: Pronouncement of blessing on forgiven sinners (cf. the Beatitudes in Matt. 5:3–12).

Verses 3–4:	The physical and spiritual exhaustion that comes from unconfessed sin.
Verse 5:	The turning point of the psalm and of the psalmist's life: full confession leads to full forgiveness.
Verses 6–7:	Invitation to others to praise, arising from the psalmist's new relationship with God.
Verses 8–10:	Offer to instruct others in this good, new way of life.
Verse 11:	Summons to praise.

Verse 5 is the midpoint, or hinge, of the psalm. When the psalmist moves from cover-up to confession, God in turn moves from judgment (v. 4a) to redemption. Note especially the emphatic "you" in verse 5c: the renewal of their relationship is God's doing, not the psalmist's. Compare the three-fold "you" in verse 7.

Note the many vivid metaphors in this psalm, including the sinner's tongue shriveled like a plant that has withered in the summer sun (v. 4b), the threat of an overwhelming flood (v. 6b), God likened to a secret hideaway (v. 7a; cf. 1 Sam. 19:2), and the stubbornness of a horse or mule (v. 9a; cf. Isa. 1:2–3).

Not to be missed is the full vocabulary for "sin" used throughout the psalm, including "sin" ("resistance, rebellion"), "transgression" ("to miss the target;" see Judg. 20:16), "guilt" (that which is "bent" or "crooked;" see Isa. 24:1; Prov. 38:6), and "deceit" ("faulty, defective;" see Hos. 7:16). In this psalm, the full ugliness of sin is exposed.

Note also the wordplay involving the Hebrew verb *kasa:* the psalmist tried to "cover up" his sin (v. 5a); upon his confession, God "covered over" (i.e., buried) his sin (v. 1b).

Finally, the contrast between the ennui of verses 3–4 and the exuberance of verse 11 could hardly be greater.

Theology and Application

At least three theological themes are prominent in this psalm, the first of which is the nature and the effects of sin. As the psalm makes clear through its broad vocabulary, sin is not simply a "mistake" or "misdeed" but is a turning away from God, a stubborn resistance to God (v. 9). Sin thus breaks our relationship with God and leads to punishment (v. 4). We then exacerbate the situation by refusing to acknowledge our responsibility, our culpability (v. 3a), with devastating, self-inflicted results (vv. 3–4). Even our bodies suffer for our self-deceptions.

The second theme is that of confession—full, honest admission of guilt ("no deceit," v. 2b) made without excuse (v. 5). Acknowledging our guilt to ourselves is a good start, but it is not enough: confession must be made to God. Such full, honest, open confession places the sinner in God's hands and thus is an expression of trust in God: confession of sin to God and profession of faith in God are two sides of the same coin. God "imputes" or "reckons" such trust as righteousness (v. 2)—as he did to Abraham (Gen. 15:6, where the same Hebrew verb *chasab* is used), so he does for us today: see Romans 4:7–8 (where Paul quotes vv. 1–2 of Ps. 32) and 1 John 1:8–9.

Now the door is open for God to act on the sinner's behalf, which is the third theme of the psalm—the free, gracious forgiveness of God (v. 5b) that completely eradicates sin and its effects (v. 1, "covered over") and that leads to a new, intimate, secure relationship with God (v. 7). It is the very nature of God to be not only just but especially forgiving (Exod. 34:6–7). "Blessed" indeed are those "whose sin has been taken away, whose transgression has been covered over" (v. 1). So now let all confessed, forgiven sinners—all who have been accounted "righteous" by God, all who are "upright in heart" (v. 11)—rejoice, be glad, and sing to the top of their lungs their praise of God.

For Those Who Sing Psalm 32

Is there anything harder to say than, "I was wrong; I have sinned; I am guilty?" In an age of denial and cover-up and "extenuating circumstances," confession of sin is not a popular option. Nor was it for this psalmist, who "remained silent" (v. 3a) for as long as he could. But guilt took its toll on him (vv. 3–4)—as guilt always does—until he confessed his sin to the Lord and received from the LORD both pardon (v. 5) and protection (vv. 6–7). What a profound encouragement to prodigal rulers (2 Sam. 12:13), to prodigal sons and daughters (Luke 15:21), to all prodigals everywhere. The "one whose sin has been taken away," the "one to whom the LORD attaches no guilt," is the one who truly is "blessed" (vv. 1–2).

Paul Watson

How Blessed Are Those

Psalm 32

Gina Shipp

Mel Witcher

Be glad in Je - hov - ah, re - joice and give praise;
be thank - ful that you are his own.
Shout loud - ly, be joy - ous that you are re - deemed
and praise him for what he has done.

Forgiveness

Psalm 32

Mark Shipp

Mark Shipp
Arr. Randy Daw

Psalm 33

Translation

1 Sing out, you righteous ones, to the Lord; it is appropriate for the upright to offer praise.
2 Praise the Lord with the lyre; with the harp sing praise to him.
3 Sing to him a new song; play beautifully[a] and shout for joy.

4 For the word of the Lord is upright. He does all things faithfully.
5 He loves righteousness and justice. The steadfast love of the Lord fills the earth.

6 By God's word the heavens were made; by the breath of his mouth, all their host.
7 He collected and dammed up the waters of the sea[b]; he put the ocean depths
into storehouses.

8 Let all the earth fear the Lord; let all humanity stand in awe of him.
9 For he spoke and it happened; he gave the order, and it appeared.[c]

10 The Lord nullifies the plans of the nations; he thwarts the schemes of the peoples.
11 The plans of the Lord stand forever; his intentions, for all generations.

12 Blessed is the nation whose God is the Lord, the people he has chosen as his heritage.

13 From heaven the Lord looks down: he sees all mankind.
14 From his established dwelling place he watches intently all who inhabit the earth—
15 he who shapes the hearts of them all, he who observes everything they do.

16 No king is ever saved by a mighty army, nor a warrior by his own great strength.
17 A horse is hopeless for deliverance; for all its great power, it will not save.

18 Look—the eye of the Lord is on those who fear him, on those who hope in his stead-
fast love,
19 to deliver them from death, and to keep them alive in time of famine.

20 We wait in hope for the Lord; he is our help and our shield.
21 For in him our hearts rejoice; in his holy name we trust.

22 Let your steadfast love rest upon us, O Lord, even as we hope in you.

[a] "Beautifully." The NIV and NRSV read "skillfully."

[b] "He collected and dammed up the waters of the sea." The NIV reads "gathered the waters of the sea *into jars*," and the NRSV reads "gathered the waters of the sea *as in a bottle*." However, in light of the imagery in Genesis 1:9-10 and Exodus 15:8, the reading "dammed up" seems preferable. Cf. also NIV footnote, "sea as into a heap."

[c] "And it appeared." One meaning of the Hebrew verb *'amad* is "arise, appear, come on the scene." While less frequent than the meaning "stand, stand firm" (as in the NIV and NRSV), "appeared" seems more appropriate in this context.

Structure and Poetry

Psalm 33 is a hymn of praise—one of the few hymns in Book I (Pss. 1–41) and Book II (Pss. 42–72) of the Psalter. The invitation to praise in 33:1 echoes the last verse of Psalm 32 and the rest of Psalm 33 responds to that invitation.

The structure and format of Psalm 33 are simple, but not simplistic. The verses come in pairs, for the most part (vv. 13–15 are an exception), with verses 1, 12, and 22 marking the beginning, mid-point, and end of the psalm:

Verse 1:	An invitation to those in a right relationship with God to celebrate that relationship.
Verses 1–3:	Such praise should be exuberant and unrestrained. For a similar sentiment, see Psalm 150:3–5.
Verses 4–5:	The motivation or reason for such praise is clear: what God says and does is perfectly consistent with who he is: faithful, just, righteous, etc.
Verses 6–7:	God's word and work began with creation. Note the echoes of Genesis 1–2: "And God said . . ." (Gen. 1:3, 6, etc.); the "host" (stars?) of heaven; (Gen. 2:1); the "deep" (Gen. 1:2); the collecting of the waters (Gen. 1:9).
Verses 8–9:	The appropriate response to God's powerful, generative word: fear and awe.
Verses 10–11:	God's lordship over all human history; his plans overrule those of all nations and peoples.
Verse 12:	A blessing on that people whom God has chosen (reflecting God's call of Abraham and subsequent covenant with Israel).
Verses 13–15:	God's ongoing "oversight" of his creatures and his world.
Verses 16–17:	The issue is broached: where does power reside in creation? Not in the typical expressions of such power—political and military might.
Verses 18–19:	Saving power comes from God alone to those who fear him and hope in him.
Verses 20–21:	Now the psalm shifts from general, universal truth to personal response: "*We* wait in hope . . . rejoice . . . trust."
Verse 22:	A concluding prayer asking for God's abiding, steadfast love.

One final literary feature of Psalm 33 should be noted, and that is its didactic nature: the psalm *teaches* as it *praises*. Although the psalm is not an acrostic, its twenty-two verses parallel the twenty-two letters of the Hebrew alphabet. The compact lines of poetry; the repetitions in the psalm ("all" in vv. 6, 8, 13, 14, 15; "great" in vv. 16–17); and the groups of five (five imperatives to praise in vv. 1–3; the five-fold description of God in vv. 4–5) are all characteristic of "wisdom" instruction, as is the emphasis on creation in verses 6–9. Thus Psalm 33 not only invites us to praise God and shows us *how* to praise God; it also reminds us who God is and why he is to be praised.

Theology and Application

The Psalms have been called "Israel's theology set to music." Psalm 33 is a prime example of this definition. Psalm 33 is not "any old song" sung to "any old God" (think Acts 17:23), but is directed to a quite specific God who has quite specific characteristics and accomplishments. Nor is the theology of Psalm 33 abstract and philosophical. Instead, it is dynamic and interactive, for it is a living LORD who is both described and honored by worshippers for whom he is both "help" and "shield" (v. 20).

Without a doubt the theological focus of Psalm 33 is the absolute sovereignty of God over both world (creation) and humanity (history). As recent hymns express it, "power, all power, surely is thine," and "How great thou art!"

Even though this God has chosen one people as his heritage (v. 12b), his sovereign reign extends over "all"—all the earth (v. 8), all generations (v. 11), all humankind (v. 13).

God's sovereignty is only, always beneficent, for God himself is "upright" and "faithful" and a lover of "righteousness" and "justice." The earth is filled with his "steadfast love" (vv. 4–5)—and that is "good news;" that is "gospel."

How should we respond to such a God? By praising him for his steadfast love today (vv. 1–3) and by waiting in hope and trust for his steadfast love tomorrow (vv. 20–22).

For Those Who Sing Psalm 33

If asked, "What is the dominant reality in our world today?" what would you say? Pollution and global warming? Poverty? Fear of "wars and rumors of wars"? Competing ideologies, both political and religious? In this hymn of praise, the psalmist declares that the dominant reality is "the steadfast love of the LORD" that "fills the earth" (v. 5b). It is the LORD God who created our world (vv. 6–7), whose intentions for our world are unwavering (vv. 10–11), who constantly watches over our world (vv. 13–15), and who pledges by his steadfast love to do what neither political skill nor military power can ever do—deliver us from death itself (vv. 16–19). How right and how good it is to pray, in all confidence, "Let your steadfast love rest upon us, O LORD, even as we hope in you" (v. 22).

Paul Watson

The Lord Is Our Hope

Psalm 33

Martha Pounders Walker

Felix Kneuper
Arr. by Randy Daw

The Lord Is Our Hope

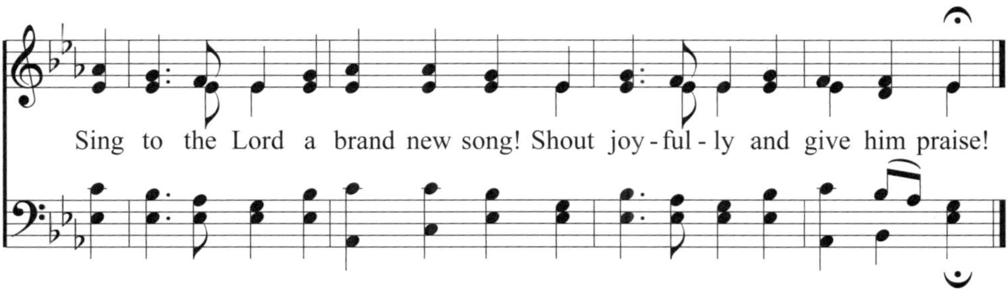

Sing Praise!

Psalm 33

Laura K. Collum | Ruth Ann Somervell

stronger
Sing praise to the Lord! He de-serves eve - ry praise. Our bless-ings in-
crease for he calls us his own. Sing prais - es to him for his
1, 2, 4
Fine
un-fail - ing love. We hope in you, Lord, and we trust you a - lone.
3
trust you a - lone. No con-quer - ing ar - my, no pow - er - ful
D.C. al Fine
king, no ar - se - nal might - y can vic - to - ry bring!

Choral

His Steadfast Love Fills All the Earth

Psalm 33

Martha Pounders Walker | M. L. Daniels

His Steadfast Love Fills All the Earth

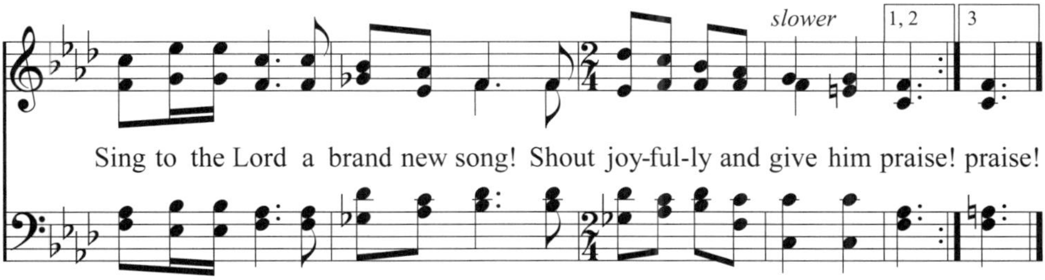

Psalm 34

Translation

Of David, when he pretended to be insane before Abimelech, who drove him out and he got away.

†1 (א, *aleph*) I will bless the Lord at all times; forever shall his praise be on my lips.
*2 (ב, *bet*) My soul will boast in the Lord; let the humble hear and rejoice.[a]
*3 (ג, *gimel*) Magnify the Lord along with me; let us lift up his name together.
†4 (ד, *dalet*) I sought the Lord, and he answered me; from all my fears he delivered me.
†5 (ה, *he* and ו, *waw*) Those who look to him radiate joy; their faces[b] never blush with shame.
†6 (ז, *zayin*) This poor one called out, and the Lord listened; and from all distress he delivered him.
†7 (ח, *het*) God's messenger encamps around those who fear him, and he saves them.
*8 (ט, *tet*) Taste and see that the Lord is good; blessed is the one who seeks refuge in him.
*9 (י, *yod*) Fear the Lord, you who are his holy ones; for those who fear him are never impoverished.
*10 (כ, *kaph*) Young lions may go poor and hungry, but those who seek the Lord never lack any good thing.

†11 (ל, *lamed*) Come, children, listen to me, and I will teach you the fear of the Lord.
†12 (מ, *mem*) Who among you enjoys life? Who longs to see good days?
†13 (נ, *nun*) Guard your tongue from evil and your lips from speaking falsehood.
†14 (ס, *samek*) Stay away from evil and do what is good; seek peace and pursue it.
†15 (ע, *ayin*) The eyes of the Lord are upon the righteous, and his ears are open to their outcries.
†16 (פ, *pe*) The face of the Lord is set against evildoers, to cut off the memory of them from the earth.
*17 (צ, *tsade*) The righteous cry out for help, and the Lord hears them; from all their troubles he rescues them.
*18 (ק, *qoph*) The Lord is near to those whose hearts are broken; he saves those whose spirits are crushed.
†19 (ר, *resh*) A righteous person may have many problems, but from them all the Lord will deliver him.
†20 (ש, *shin*) He protects all his bones—not one of them will be broken.

†21 (ת, *taw*) Evil brings death to those who are evil, and those who hate the righteous will themselves be found guilty.

*22 (פ, *pe*) The LORD redeems the life of his servants; all who take refuge in him will be found innocent.

[a] "Let the humble hear and rejoice." The NRSV also reads "humble," while the NIV has "afflicted." The former seems preferable, especially in light of "This poor man (NIV) / soul (NRSV) . . ." in verse 6.

[b] "Their faces." The NIV shares this translation. Based on Greek and Syriac renderings, the NRSV reads "your faces."

Structure and Poetry

Psalm 34 is best heard as a song of thanksgiving for deliverance from some unspecified threat (vv. 4 and 6). While praising God for his deliverance, the psalmist clearly invites others to experience God's salvation for themselves—he longs for others to share his experience with God (vv. 2–3, 8–9).

Psalm 34, like Psalm 25, is also a true acrostic: each verse begins with a successive letter of the Hebrew alphabet. [The letter *waw* begins the second half of v. 5; and v. 22 repeats the letter *pe.*] The lines of the psalm are regular and compact, and the words of the psalm are among the most common in the Hebrew vocabulary. Together with other features—e.g., the invitation to learn (v. 11) and the exhortations to "fear" the LORD (vv. 7, 9, 11) and live ethically (vv. 13–14)—this suggests a *didactic* as well as a *liturgical* function of the psalm: it was composed both for *worship* and for *instruction*.

Although other outlines have been suggested, the simplest is as follows:

Verses 1–10: An invitation to praise God, based on the psalmist's own experience of God's protection (v. 7), goodness (v. 8), and provision of "daily bread" (v. 10).

Verses 11–20: The way of life that will elicit God's continued attention (v. 15), rescue (v. 17), nearness (v. 18), and protection (v. 20).

Verses 21–22: The ultimate verdicts: on evildoers—"guilty"; but on the righteous, God's servants—"innocent."

Theology and Application

Of all the theological affirmations of Psalm 34, both explicit and implicit, five stand out:

First, God's compassionate concern for those who are alone and afraid (v. 4), who are in need (v. 10), whose hearts are broken (v. 18). One cannot help but think of Jesus' assurances: "blessed are the poor in spirit . . . those who mourn . . . the meek . . . those who hunger and thirst after righteousness" (Matt. 5:3–6). The cries of the helpless and the hopeless do not turn God away, but rather turn him toward those who need him and cry out to him (v. 15).

Second, this compassionate God is also a powerful God who can and will deliver/protect/acquit those who call upon him (vv. 4, 6, 7, 8b, 10b, 17, 19, 20, 22)—those who, by the power of God, are "more than conquerors" (Rom. 8:31–39).

Third, our experience of the powerful, compassionate presence of God in our lives becomes the basis for our own praise and thanksgiving (vv. 1–2a) and for our invitation to others to join us in praising God (vv. 2b–3, 8–9). Our praise for God springs not (or, not primarily) from our rational comprehension of God, but from our ongoing relationship with God—and thus we invite others to "come, taste and see" (v. 8; cf. John 1:46 and Philip's response to Nathaniel's doubt about Jesus being the Messiah: "come and see").

Fourth, the powerful compassion of God becomes the basis not only for our worship, but also for our ethics. Our "fear of the LORD" (vv. 9, 11)—if it is genuine—will inevitably lead us into a pattern of behavior such as is summarized in vv. 13–14: ". . . stay away from evil and do what is good."

Finally, the psalm does not promise a care-free life to the "righteous" who "seek" God both in worship and in daily living, but just the opposite: "a righteous person may have many problems" (v. 19a). Instead, the promise is for strength to bear the trials of life, for patience to endure hardship, and for ultimate deliverance: "but from them all, the LORD will deliver him" (v. 19b).

For Those Who Sing Psalm 34

Our greatest joy is the joy that we share with others. To see a beautiful sunset, to hear a majestic symphony, to find a new friend—these and other such joys are enhanced when we tell others about them. So it was with this psalmist. Insignificant though he may have been, he "called out, and the LORD listened" and answered his cry for help (v. 6). Yet he was not unique, for when "the righteous cry out for help, . . . the LORD hears them" (v. 17a). The LORD is not put off by "those whose hearts are broken . . . those whose spirits are crushed" (v. 18); indeed, those are the very ones whom God "delivers" and "saves" (v. 7). Have you known the joy of God's compassionate presence? If so, "let us lift up his name together" (v. 3b). If not, come "taste and see that the LORD is good" (v. 8a).

Paul Watson

Taste and See That the Lord Is Good

Psalm 34

Jack R. Reese | Jack R. Reese

Taste and See That the Lord Is Good

I Bless the Lord Both Day and Night

Psalm 34

Mark Shipp | Konstantin Zhigulin

I Bless the Lord Both Day and Night

Psalm 35

Translation

Of David.

1 Contend, O Lord, against those who contend with me; do battle with those who fight against me!
2 Take up shield and armor, and rise up to help me!
3 Uncover spear and weapon against my pursuers; say to me, "I am your salvation."
4 May those who seek my life be dishonored and disgraced; may those who intend to harm me recoil with shame.
5 Let them be like chaff before the wind; let the angel of the Lord drive them away.
6 Let their way be dark and slippery; let the angel of the Lord drive them on.
7 For without cause they set their net to trap me; without cause they dug a pit for me.
8 Let ruin come upon them unexpectedly; let the net that they set for me capture them; let them fall into it[a]—to their own ruin.
9 Then my soul will rejoice in the Lord; I will take delight in his deliverance.
10 All my bones shall say, "O Lord, who is like you? You rescue the weak from those who overpower them, the weak and the needy from those who take advantage of them."

11 Violent witnesses come forward; they ask me things I know nothing about.
12 They repay me evil for good; they leave me empty.
13 Yet, when they were ill, I put on sackcloth. I humbled myself by fasting, but my prayer came back unanswered.[b]
14 As for a friend, as for my own brother, I walked about like someone lamenting his mother, wearing funeral clothes, bowed down with grief.
15 But when I stumbled, they got together and laughed; they ganged up on me—oppressors whom I did not even know—they tore into me and never stopped.
16 They mocked me unmercifully[c]; they gnashed their teeth over me.
17 O Lord, how long will you watch? Rescue me from their assaults, my very being from these young lions.
18 I will give you thanks in the great assembly; among a throng of people will I sing your praise.

19 Do not allow my enemies to rejoice over me unreasonably, or those who hate me undeservedly to wink their eyes.
20 For they do not pronounce peace; instead, they devise deceitful words against those who live quietly in the land.
21 They open wide their mouths against me; they say, "Aha! Aha! Our eyes have seen it."

22 You have seen all this, O LORD; don't be silent. O LORD, do not distance yourself from me.
23 Wake up, and come to my defense, my God, my LORD—take up my case!
24 Acquit me, according to your righteousness, O LORD my God, and do not allow them to rejoice on my account.
25 Do not let them say to themselves, "Aha! Just what we wanted." Do not let them say, "We have eaten him alive."
26 Instead, let them all be ashamed and humiliated—those who rejoice over my misfortune. Let them be clothed with shame and dishonor—those who exalt themselves over me.
27 Let those who delight in my righteousness shout with joy and rejoice; let them always say, "The LORD be exalted—he who delights in the well-being of his servant."
28 My own tongue shall proclaim your righteousness and shall praise you all day long.

[a] "Let them fall into it." The NIV takes "it" to be the "pit" of verse 7, while the NRSV takes it to be the "net" (also v. 7).

[b] "But my prayer came back unanswered." This translation agrees with the NIV. The NRSV reads, "I prayed with head bowed on my bosom."

[c] "They mocked me unmercifully." This is a very difficult phrase to translate. The Hebrew may mean "ungodly circle of mockers" (as in the NIV footnote) or "like the profanest mockers of a cake" (as in the NRSV footnote).

Structure and Poetry

Psalm 35 is the prolonged, passionate prayer of a faithful person in a desperate situation and in dire need of God's help. As such, it has all the characteristics of an "individual lament," including a description of the trouble or need of the psalmist; a petition to God to hear and to help; reasons why God should respond; expressions of confidence in God's favorable response; and a promise to worship and praise God for his (anticipated) deliverance.

While there is no standard order in the lament psalms for these separate parts, Psalm 35 has three rather clear units, each of which moves toward God's praise:

Verses 1–10: Strong petitions for deliverance, ending in the promised praise of verses 9–10.

Verses 11–18: The psalmist's innocence contrasted with his enemies' guilt, again moving to a vow to "give you thanks in the great assembly" (v. 18).

Verses 19–28: More strong petitions for God to act on the psalmist's behalf, vindicating him while finding his enemies guilty, with a final promise to praise (v. 28).

While metaphors of warfare (vv. 1–3) and hunting (vv. 7–8) appear in the psalm, the predominant imagery is that of the law-court, from "contend, O LORD" (literally, "go to court on my behalf," v. 1a) to "violent witnesses" (v. 11) to "come to my defense" and "acquit me" (vv. 23–24). Whether the courtroom metaphor is to be taken literally—the psalmist has been falsely accused and is on trial for his life—or figuratively, it is a powerful, compelling picture of a righteous person unable to defend or extricate himself from some dire situation.

Other vivid words and phrases include windblown chaff (v. 5; cf. Ps. 1:4), ravenous young lions (v. 17), a dark, slippery passageway (v. 6), gnashing teeth (v. 16), sly winks (v. 19), and sackcloth and fasting (v. 13). The word "ruin" in verse 8 is the Hebrew word *sho'ah,* now used to designate the Jewish Holocaust. Contrasted with this "ruin" is the "peace, well-being" (Hebrew *shalom*) withheld by the enemies (v. 20) but granted by God (v. 27).

Theology and Application

Psalm 35 struggles with the still-current problem of undeserved evil (v. 19). It was the case for the psalmist—as for many today—that sympathy and solidarity with others (vv. 13–14) are often "repaid," not with commensurate acts of kindness, but with "evil" (v. 12). A righteous person may well be falsely accused (v. 19) in a matter he/she knows nothing about (v. 11). A righteous person may be "ganged-up on" by unknown opponents (v. 15), "mocked unmercifully" (v. 16), or lied about (vv. 20–21). As Jesus himself said, quoting verse 19, "They hated me without reason." Undeserved evil—unreasonable hatred—is very real.

How is a "righteous" person to respond to such personal and potentially deadly attacks? This psalmist demands that God intervene: "Wake up, and come to my defense." This is no abstract theological reflection about the constant alertness of God, but rather the urgent personal demand of one who *knows* a) that Jehovah God is a God who takes his stand with the poor and needy, and thus is like no other god (v. 10), and b) that God's only desire is for the "well-being" (*shalom*) of his "servants" (v. 27). Even when we hit rock-bottom, we find God there waiting and willing to help us.

But what of the psalmist's plea not only for personal vindication, but also for divine retribution on his enemies (vv. 8, 26)? Some would say that Christ's command, "Love your enemies" (Matt. 5:44) supersedes this plea. But others would point out that God's vindication of the righteous inevitably entails his judgment upon the wicked. To find the righteous innocent is to find those who have mocked the righteous, and who have plotted harm against them, guilty. To seek such vindication is to pray, "Thy will be done on earth, as it is in heaven" and "deliver us from evil," and to anticipate the enactment of Jesus' promise, "all who exalt themselves will be humbled, but all who humble themselves will be exalted" (Luke 18:14).

For Those Who Sing Psalm 35

Rightly or wrongly, court cases are often won or lost, not on the basis of the evidence, but on the skill and dedication of the lawyer who argues the case. Thus, without competent legal counsel, an innocent person may be found guilty. The earnest request of this psalmist is for the LORD to take his case and defend him from "those who hate me undeservedly" (v. 19) and who seek to do him harm (vv. 15–16, 19–21). This we can understand and replicate in similar situations of our own. But can we defend the psalmist's further request that his oppressors fall into their own trap (v. 8)—that they "get what's coming to them"? We can, if with the psalmist we leave their judgment to God and simply pray, "Thy will be done on earth as it is in heaven."

Paul Watson

Contend, O Lord, Contend

Psalm 35

Mark Shipp | M. L. Daniels

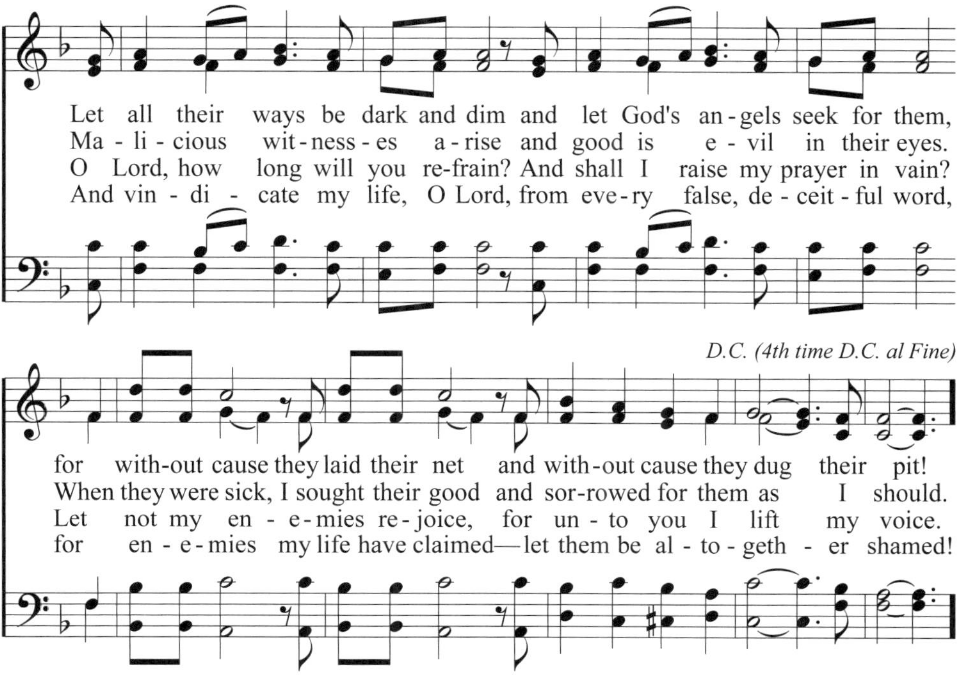
Let all their ways be dark and dim and let God's an-gels seek for them,
Ma - li - cious wit-ness - es a - rise and good is e - vil in their eyes.
O Lord, how long will you re-frain? And shall I raise my prayer in vain?
And vin - di - cate my life, O Lord, from eve-ry false, de - ceit - ful word,
D.C. (4th time D.C. al Fine)
for with-out cause they laid their net and with-out cause they dug their pit!
When they were sick, I sought their good and sor-rowed for them as I should.
Let not my en - e-mies re-joice, for un - to you I lift my voice.
for en - e-mies my life have claimed—let them be al - to - geth - er shamed!

Contend, O Lord

Adapted from Psalm 35

Michael R. Greene

Michael R. Greene

Contend, O Lord

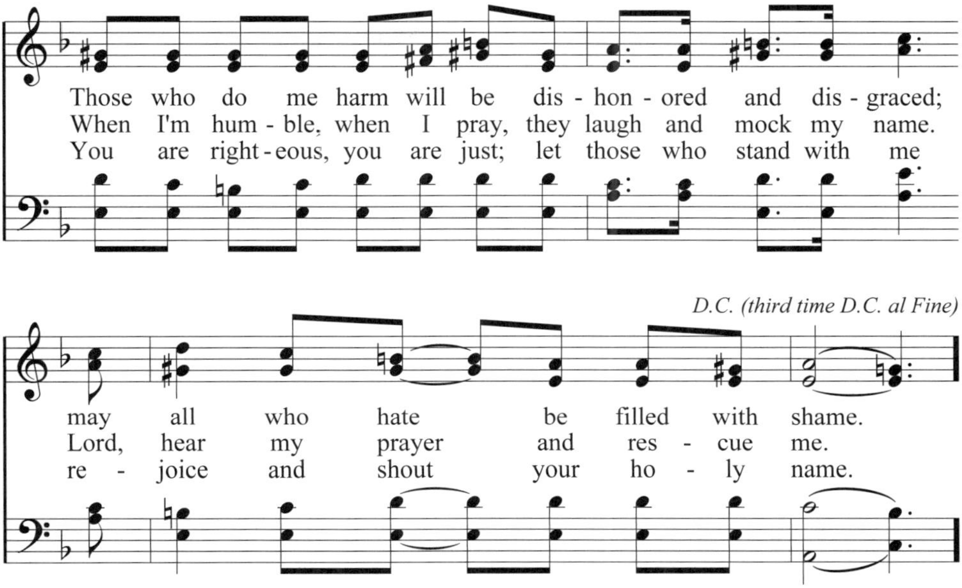

Psalm 36

Translation

For the director. Of the servant of the LORD, of David.

1 An oracle: Transgression belongs to the wicked in the midst of his heart.[a] He has no
fear of God before his eyes.
2 Because in his own eyes he flatters himself, he refuses to acknowledge his iniquity.

3 The words of his mouth are wicked and deceitful; he no longer[b] acts with wisdom
or goodness.
4 He plans wicked things on his bed; he is set on a way that is not good; he does not
reject evil.

5 O LORD, your steadfast love *reaches* into the heavens, your faithfulness to the clouds.
6 Your righteousness is like the mighty mountains, your justice like the great deep. You
deliver humans and beasts, O LORD.
7 How precious is your steadfast love! The mighty and lowly[c] find refuge in the shadow
of your wings.
8 They feast on the rich abundance of your house, and you give them drink from the river
of your delights.
9 For with you is the fountain of life, and in your light, we see light.

10 Continue your steadfast love to those who know you, and your righteousness to the
upright of heart.
11 Do not let the foot of the arrogant come against me, nor the hand of the wicked drive
me away.

12 There they fall, those who do wicked things, thrown down and unable to rise.

[a] The Hebrew of verses 1–2 is ambiguous. Translations vary widely.

[b] Literally, "he has ceased to do wise, to do good."

[c] Literally, "gods and the sons of man." The word "god" sometimes denotes the powerful, so the idea may essentially be, "the powerful and the lowly."

Structure and Poetry

Psalm 36 exhibits characteristics of Lament and Wisdom Psalms. Lament: the description of the wicked (vv. 1–4) and the request that God act against these opponents (vv. 10–12). Wisdom: key ideas and phrases such as "fear of God" (v. 1), "flatters himself in his own eyes" (v. 2), and the term "wisdom" (v. 3).

The poet organizes the psalm in three sections: 1) a descriptive warning about the danger the wicked pose to the community (vv. 1–4), 2) descriptive praise of the Lord who provides refuge to the community (vv. 5–9), and 3) a request that the Lord will again act in favor of the righteous, against the wicked (vv. 10–12).

Theology and Application

In the first section, the psalmist uses body imagery to describe the wicked and the depth of their corruption: the *heart* has transgression deep within (v. 1); the *eyes* do not look in reverence toward God (no fear of God), but look to the self in flattery (v. 1); the *mouth* speaks only wicked and deceptive words (v. 2). Wickedness infects every part of the body. Further, this person has no desire to get well. He is too much in love with himself to see his mistakes (v. 2), and he is "set on a way that is not good" (v. 4). As a result, the wicked person is not only self-destructive, but a danger to the community. He "no longer acts with wisdom or goodness" (v. 3), but casually and persistently plans the next "wicked thing" (v. 4).

In contrast to the wicked, the psalmist proclaims the essential and defining traits of the Lord: steadfast love, faithfulness, righteousness, and justice (vv. 5–6; cf. Exod. 34:6–7). The Lord's love and faithfulness are far-reaching, from the heavens and clouds (v. 5) to the depths of the oceans (v. 6), while his righteousness exhibits the strength and stability of mighty mountains (v. 6).

The Lord's character finds concrete expression in his help for all: humans and beasts (v. 6) and the mighty and lowly (v. 7). Extravagant and unreserved, the Lord's deliverance provides far more than refuge or safety. Those rescued by the Lord feast on the riches of his abundance and drink from the river of his delights (the "fountain of life," vv. 8–9). They see light because they are in the Lord's light (v. 9).

Based on the contrast between the wicked (vv. 1–4) and the extravagant love of God (vv. 5–9), the psalmist asks that God's love remain for those who seek and have relationship with him ("know you," v. 10). The psalmist asks that God not allow the proud and wicked to keep him away from God's presence (v. 11). Confidently, the poet envisions that the wicked will collapse, unable to stand against him or anyone else (v. 12).

Implicitly, the psalmist also pushes the reader to ask: With whom does my identity belong? Do I behave like the wicked: self-absorbed, self-deceived, and set on a destructive trajectory? Or am I more like the Lord: faithful and just, with steadfast love that reaches out to those in need? Psalm 36 reminds us, as we appeal for God's support, that our character reveals our true identity, whether we belong to the Lord or ourselves.

For Those Who Sing Psalm 36

Consider a contrast. On one side is the self-asserting, self-congratulatory person who always has a plan to take advantage of others. On the other side is a God whose love has no limits. Extravagant and unreserved, the LORD's deliverance from the wicked provides us more than mere safety. Those rescued by the LORD feast on the riches of his abundance and drink from the river of his delights.

Glenn Pemberton

Your Steadfast Love Is Higher Far

Psalm 36

Glover Shipp, Mark Shipp, & Heath Jones

Heath Jones
Arr. M. L. Daniels

How Precious Is Your Steadfast Love

Adapted from Psalm 36:5–10

Clyde H. Slimp

Clyde H. Slimp
Arr. M. L. Daniels

reach - es to the skies. O Lord, your
right - eous - ness is like maj - es - tic moun - tains. You re-
1
2
D.C. al Coda
fresh us from your riv - er of de - lights. de - lights.
Lord, we praise you for your stead - fast love.

Psalm 37

Translation

Of David.
1 (א, *aleph*) Do not worry about evil people; do not envy those doing wrong,
2 for like grass they will suddenly wither; like sprigs of green they will fade away.

3 (ב, *bet*) Trust in the Lord and do good; dwell in the land and enjoy safe pasture.
4 Delight in the Lord and he will give you your heart's desire.

5 (ג, *gimel*) Commit your way to the Lord; trust him and he will act.
6 He will make your vindication shine like light and justice for you like the noonday sun.

7 (ד, *dalet*) Be still before the Lord; wait patiently for him. Do not worry about the suc-
cessful, those who carry out schemes.

8 (ה, *he*) Avoid anger and abandon wrath; do not worry—it only leads to evil.
9 For those who do evil will be destroyed, but those who wait for the Lord will inherit
the land.

10 (ו, *waw*) Only a little time and the wicked will be gone; you will search for their place,
but they will not be there.
11 The humble will inherit the land and delight in abundant peace.

12 (ז, *zayin*) The wicked plot against the righteous and bare their teeth against them.
13 The Lord laughs at them, for he sees that their day is coming.

14 (ח, *het*) The wicked draw their sword and bend their bows to bring down the poor and
weak, to slaughter the upright.
15 Their sword will pierce their own heart, and their bows will be shattered.

16 (ט, *tet*) Better is the little that the righteous have than the great wealth of the wicked.
17 For the strength of the wicked will be shattered, but the Lord sustains the righteous.

18 (י, *yod*) The Lord knows the days of the blameless; their heritage will last forever.
19 They will not be shamed in adverse times; in days of famine they will have abundance.

20 (כ, *kaph*) For the wicked will perish—the enemies of the Lord—; like the best pasture
land they will vanish; they will vanish like smoke.

21 (ל, *lamed*) The wicked borrow and never repay, but the righteous are gracious and
generous.

22 Those they bless will possess the land, but those they curse will be destroyed.

23 (מ, *mem*) The LORD establishes a person's steps; he takes pleasure in his way.
24 If he falls, he will not fall flat, for the LORD holds his hand.

25 (נ, *nun*) I was young and now am old, but I have not seen the righteous abandoned or their children looking for food.
26 Every day they are gracious and lend; their offspring become a blessing.
27 (ס, *samek*) Turn from evil and do good and live securely forever,
28 for the LORD loves justice and he will not abandon his faithful ones.
(ע, *ayin*) They will be kept forever,[a] but the offspring of the wicked will be destroyed.

29 The righteous will possess the land, and they will live in it forever.

30 (פ, *pe*) The mouth of the righteous utters wisdom, and their tongue speaks justice.
31 The teaching of their God is in their heart, and their steps do not slip.

32 (צ, *tsade*) The wicked wait to ambush the righteous and seek to kill them.
33 The LORD will not abandon them into their hand, or let them be judged guilty when on trial.

34 (ק, *qoph*) Wait for the LORD and keep his way. He will exalt you to possess the land; you will see the wicked destroyed.

35 (ר, *resh*) I have seen violent, wicked people flourishing like a well-watered tree.
36 Then I passed by[b] and they were gone; I looked for them, but they were not to be found.

37 (ש, *shin*) Observe the blameless, look at the upright, for a person of peace has a future.
38 But transgressors will be completely destroyed, for destruction is the future of the wicked.

39 (ת, *taw*) Deliverance of the righteous comes from the LORD, their strength in times of trouble.
40 The LORD helps them and rescues them; he rescues them from the wicked and saves them, because they take refuge in him.

[a] There is some debate about the original text of this line. Some suggest that the text is corrupt and should read, "The unjust will be destroyed forever." Since the Hebrew makes sense in the context, I have read with the Hebrew.

[b] Reading first person (with the Septuagint) rather than third person (with the Hebrew).

Structure and Poetry

Psalm 37 is an acrostic. Beginning with the first letter of the Hebrew alphabet (*aleph*) each two-verse unit begins with the consecutive letter, concluding with the final letter (*taw*) in verse 39. As a result of the acrostic form, the poem may seem at times less coherent than non-acrostic psalms or somewhat disconnected as it moves from line to line. The difficulty in achieving a smooth acrostic composition is understandable (in this volume, see other acrostics in Pss. 9–10, 25, and 34).

Theology and Application

The primary theme of the psalm is placing trust in the LORD rather than worrying about the success of the wicked. Several times, the psalm urges the reader not to worry (vv. 1, 7, 8), but to trust in the LORD (vv. 3, 5, 7, 34). The balance of the psalm gives reasons for such trust without worry. On the one hand, the wicked will fade away (v. 2) and kill themselves in their efforts to hurt others (vv. 14–15); their strength will be shattered (v. 17). They will perish like smoke (v. 20), their offspring will be destroyed (v. 28b), they will vanish or disappear (vv. 10, 35–36), and they will be completely destroyed (vv. 9, 22, 38). The LORD laughs at the wicked (v. 13).

On the other hand, those who trust in the LORD will enjoy safe pasture (v. 3), receive their heart's desire (v. 4), be vindicated by the LORD (v. 6), delight in abundant peace or prosperity (v. 11), and be sustained by the LORD (v. 17). They will inherit and possess the land (vv. 9, 11, 22, 29, 34), not fall beyond help (v. 24), live securely (vv. 27, 28), and have a bright future (v. 37). In all of these matters, it is the LORD who blesses the righteous (those who trust him).

Then and now, it often seems like those who succeed are the wicked, those who live for themselves and take advantage of others, while those who trust in God finish last. Such appearances can be disheartening to those trying to live for God. Psalm 37 claims that this is merely an appearance, not reality. Those who trust God are truly blessed, while the wicked ultimately fail. So the psalmist calls upon the reader to trust God and wait for God to act, rather than to worry. Worry is the external evidence of a lack of trust in the LORD to be faithful (vv. 23–24, 28, 33), to vindicate (v. 6), to sustain (v. 17), and to help and rescue us (v. 40).

The psalmist's extreme claim in verse 25 ("I have not seen the righteous abandoned") should be tempered with counter-claims in other canonical writings (e.g., Job 21:7–26). This psalmist may not have seen the righteous in need or their children begging for food, but others see this happen throughout the world. In response, the righteous should be "gracious and lend" to those in need (v. 26).

For Those Who Sing Psalm 37

It is disheartening, but so often it seems like only those who live for themselves get ahead in life. Those who trust in God finish last or don't even finish the race at all. While Paul reminds us that we do not live only for this world, this psalmist reminds us that despite appearances, our God is trustworthy—here and now. This does not mean guarantees of wealth for every believer, but it leads us to a deep longing for courage and faith that sets aside our worries and waits patiently and confidently for our God.

Glenn Pemberton

Do Not Worry about Evil People

Psalm 37

Chant

Translation by Glenn Pemberton

Mel Witcher

6. Bet—ter is the little that the righteous have, than the great wealth of the wick—ed.
For the strength of the wicked will be shattered but the Lord sustains the right—eous.
The Lord knows the days of the blameless, their heritage will last for— ev—er.
They will not be shamed in adverse times; in days of famine they will have a- bund—ance.

7. For the wicked will perish—the enemies of the Lord;
like the best pasture land they will vanish—they will vanish like smoke.
The wick—ed borrow and never repay, but the righteous are gracious and gen—erous.
Those they bless will possess the land, but those they curse will be de— stroyed.

8. The Lord establishes a person's steps, he takes pleasure in his way.
If he falls, he will not fall flat, for the Lord holds his hand.
I am old, but I have not seen the righteous or their children looking for food.
Eve—ry day they are gracious and lend; their offspring become a bles—sing.

9. Turn from evil and do good and live securely for— ev—er.
For the Lord loves justice and he will not abandon his faith—ful ones.
They will be kept forever, but the offspring of the wicked will be de— stroyed.
The righteous will possess the land and they will live in it for— ev—er.

10. The mouth of the righteous utters wisdom and their tongue speaks jus—tice.
The teaching of their God is in their heart and their steps do not slip.
The wicked wait to ambush the righteous and seek to kill them.
The Lord will not abandon them, or let them be judged when on tri—al.

11. Wait for the Lord and keep his way. He will exalt you to possess the land;
You will see the wicked de— stroyed.
I have seen violent, wicked people flourishing like a well-watered tree.
Then I passed by and they were gone, looked, but they were not to be found.

12. Observe the blameless, look at the upright, for a person of peace has a fu—ture.
But trans— gressors will be destroyed, for destruction is the future of the wick—ed.
De— liver-ance comes from the Lord, their strength in times of trou—ble.
The Lord rescues them from the wicked because they take refuge in him.

Trust in the Lord

Psalm 37

Marva L. Hughes | Marva L. Hughes

for the hum - ble shall in - her - it their land and dwell in peace.
While the Lord sus - tains the right - eous, his strength he will im - part.
with a her - i - tage for - ev - er, shall they poss - ess the land!
he re - mains, for all the faith - ful, their ref - uge and their stay.
God the Lord will be their res - cue, their help in times of woe.
in the land that he has prom - ised to dwell for - ev - er - more.
Trust in the Lord, he will de - liv - er! Your heart's de - sire he will ful - fill.
molto rit.
In him de - light, his hand will guide you; wait for the Lord, in him be still.

Trust Your Ways unto Jehovah

Psalm 37, an alphabetic acrostic

Mark Shipp & Jerry Shipp

Randy Daw & Mark Shipp

Trust Your Ways unto Jehovah

Psalm 38

Translation

A song of David, for the memorial offering.
*1 O Lord, rebuke me not in your anger; correct me not in your wrath.

†2 Ah, your arrows have pierced me; your hand has come down hard on me.
*3 My flesh has no health because of your indignation; my bones have no wholeness because of my sin.

†4 Ah, my iniquities have piled up over my head, a burden too heavy for me.
†5 My wounds fester and stink because of my follies.
†6 I am bent, stooped so low; all day long—darkness—I walk.

†7 Ah, my loins are filled with burning pain; my flesh has no health.
†8 I am numb, completely crushed; I cry from the groaning within my heart.

*9 O Master, all my desire is known to you; my sighing is not hidden from you.
*10 My heart stutters; my strength abandons me; my sight even fails me.
*11 My friends and my companions stand away from my affliction; those close to me stand far away.

*12 Those seeking my life lay their traps, those wanting to hurt me discuss destruction; they plan deception all day long.

*13 But I am like the deaf, who cannot hear; like the mute, who cannot speak.
*14 Indeed, I am like a person who cannot hear, and who has no response in my mouth.

†15 Ah, it is for you, O Lord, I wait; it is you who will answer, O Master my God.

†16 Ah, I said, "Only do not let them rejoice over me, or when my feet stumble they will boast against me."

†17 Ah, I go on limping and limping, my pain always the next step before me.

†18 Ah, I confess my iniquity, I am troubled by my sin.

†19 I have so many foes without cause; so many who hate me for no reason.
†20 They repay evil for good; they are my adversaries though I pursue what is good.

*21 O Lord, do not abandon me! O my God, do not be so far from me!
*22 Hurry to my aid, O Master, my Savior.

Structure and Poetry

While direct appeals to God ("O Lord") provide some structural divisions to the psalm (vv. 1, 9, 15, 21, 22), the poet's object of concern provides additional shape: God's violent actions (vv. 1–3a), the psalmist's failures and suffering (vv. 3b–10), the response from others (vv. 11–12), the psalmist's inability to respond to their threats (vv. 13–14), and finally the psalmist's direct appeal to God—including vivid re-description of his pain, his sin, his enemies, and his need for God's presence (vv. 15–22).

Theology and Application

Psalm 38 is an intense lament with all the typical components of this form. First, the psalmist addresses the Lord with words in the singular throughout the psalm (e.g. O Lord, Master, my God). Second, the poet describes his condition and troubles. Health concerns overwhelm the psalmist: his flesh and bones lack health (v. 3), his wounds fester and stink (v. 5), he is stooped and bent over (v. 6), his loins burn (v. 7), he has heart palpitations, loss of strength, loss of eyesight (v. 10), and he limps in pain (v. 17). Though it is possible that one person could suffer all of these problems, we should read at least some of the complaints as metaphorical rather than literal. Nonetheless, physical problems are only one facet of the psalmist's troubles; the poet also describes social, psychological, and theological problems. Social: enemies take advantage of his situation and speak lies (vv. 12, 16, 20) and return evil for good (v. 20); friends have abandoned the psalmist at his greatest moment of need (v. 10). Psychological: he is numb and crushed by the weight of his problems (v. 8), walking in darkness (v. 6), groaning and sighing (vv. 8, 9). Theological: God is the ultimate object of complaint. Despite the psalmist's request, he feels that God has acted in anger, shot the psalmist with divine arrows, and slapped down the psalmist with the divine hand (vv. 1–2).

Third, the psalmist asks God to act in specific ways. First he requests that God stop hurting him and responding in anger (vv. 1–3). God should return to his own true self, "slow to anger, and abounding in steadfast love and faithfulness" (Exod. 34:6). Then the psalmist asks for God's attention and an answer to his prayer (v. 16). The poet requests that God not abandon him, that he not be so far away, and that he respond quickly (v. 22).

Fourth, the psalmist endeavors to motivate God to action throughout the psalm. The psalmist acknowledges his sin (vv. 3, 19); he admits that it has piled up over his head, a burden too heavy to carry (v. 4). The poet portrays his condition in the strongest possible terms in order to elicit God's compassion. His health is failing; enemies are acting unfairly, returning good deeds for bad (v. 21). The psalmist refuses to take matters into his own hands, perhaps because he is unable. Perhaps he cannot hear what his opponents are saying and so cannot speak a rebuke in reply (vv. 14–15). Or better, the psalmist is waiting for God to answer them (v. 16). The psalmist is placing all his hope on God (vv. 9, 16, 22–23). If God does not come through, there is no other plan.

Remarkably, though the psalmist identifies God as the problem at the beginning of the psalm (vv. 1–3), at the end of the psalm the poet expresses confident hope in God (vv. 9, 16, 22–23). If prayer is to be honest and the relationship authentic, these words of accusation, complaint, and grief must be spoken. This is not because of a lack of faith, but because a relationship with God requires that one speak the bold language of lament.

For Those Who Sing Psalm 38

Psalm 38 is an intense lament in its description of lost physical and mental health, lost friends, vicious enemies, and a God who has inexplicably lashed out in anger. This week, your experience of life may be far removed from this psalm. But across the room and across the world, many believers identify more with this lament than any other psalm in the book. Their lives are on the line. If God does not respond, there is no hope. So if not for yourself, read this prayer today for the sake of these others, fellow believers who may not even be able to speak for themselves. Next week, they may pick up this psalm for us—and so fulfill the law of Christ.

Glenn Pemberton

Do Not Abandon Me

(congregational version)

Psalm 38

Jack R. Reese — Jack R. Reese

Do Not Abandon Me

Psalm 38

Jack R. Reese

Jack R. Reese

limp - ing on, my pain piercing like a sword. My sin is be -
heart be - trays me, my strength is not my own. My friends once
bove my head, a bur - den all day long. My heart is
yearn for you. Quick - en me, my God. My strength is
fore me al - ways; I con-fess my in - iq - ui - ty. Come hur-ry to my
dear en - dure not here; I wait im-pa-tient-ly. Please
hushed, my spir - it crushed, I cry un-end-ing-ly. Come
tak - en, joy for - sak - en, hope I can-not see. My sa - vior,

aid; re-main with me; stay near, O Lord; do not a - ban - don me.
come to my aid; stay near, O Lord; do not a - ban - don me.
to my aid; stay near, O Lord; do not a - ban - don me.
come; stay near, O Lord; do not a - ban - don me.
last time only
Come near, O Lord; I wait for you, my mas-ter and my God.
Come near, O Lord; I wait for you, my mas-ter and my God.
Come near, O Lord; I wait for you, my mas-ter and my God.
Come near, O Lord; I wait for you, my mas-ter and my God.

Still I Wait, O Lord

Psalm 38

Jeremy Daw & Randy Daw

Randy Daw

Still I Wait, O Lord

Psalm 39

Translation

For the director. Of Jeduthun. A song of David.

1 I said, "I will guard my words so I do not sin with my tongue. I will restrain my mouth
with a muzzle while the wicked are in my presence."

2 So I was mute and silent; I was quiet for no good reason! But when my pain was stirred up,
3 my heart grew hot within me. In my groaning a fire ignited so I spoke with my tongue:

4 "Tell me, O Lord, my end. What is the measure of my days? I know I am mortal.
5 Look, you set my days with mere hand-widths; my lifetime is nothing before you.
All humanity together is only a vapor." [*Selah*]

6 People walk about as mere images; they heap up wealth, mere vapor; they don't even
know who will collect it.
7 Now, Master, what is my hope? My hope is set on you!
8 Save me from all my sins; don't make me the fool's jest.
9 I am mute; I will not open my mouth, for you have taken action.
10 Stop beating me; I am finished by the hostility of your hand.
11 You discipline a person with rebukes of iniquity; you consume his desires like a moth.
All humanity is only vapor. [*Selah*]

12 Hear my prayer, O Lord, and listen to my cry for help; do not be silent to my tears, for
I am an alien with you, a sojourner like all my ancestors.
13 Look away from me, so I may be cheerful before I go and am no more.

Structure and Poetry

Psalm 39 is a bitter lament. In the opening verses, the poet describes his futile efforts to resist voicing his complaint (vv. 1–2). His continued pain or distress, however, was like a fire burning within him, becoming hotter and hotter until finally, like a fire exploding, he says, "I spoke with my tongue" (v. 3). His attempt at silence came for two reasons: first, the potential misunderstanding by the wicked of what he would say (v. 2), and second, he did not want to implicate or indict God, though God is to blame (v. 9b). Verses 4–13 record the poet's unintended lament (it is also possible to read vv. 4–5 as the original lament with vv. 6–13 as the poet's new reflection). The lament begins with two descriptive complaints about the brevity of human life (vv. 4–5 and v. 6). Then once the poet affirms the LORD as "my hope" (v. 7), he makes passionate requests to God for help (vv. 8–11), with a final desperate appeal for the LORD to either respond to his cry or "look away from me" so that he might have some joy before he dies (vv. 12–13).

Theology and Application

Faith demands that the poet speak the truth, the whole truth, and nothing but the truth, even if the truth brings God into question. God has made human life short—just a few "handbreadths" or a "vapor" (*hebel*, the same term used in Ecclesiastes for "vanity"). In relation to God, human lifetime is nothing (vv. 5–6). Yet people live at a frenetic pace to "heap up wealth" without any apparent awareness that they will leave it all behind to someone they do not even know (v. 7). The underlying problem and reason the poet did not want to speak comes out in verse 9: God is responsible. More, the psalmist feels that God is beating him senseless and exhausting him. The poet knows that God punishes humans for sin (v. 11), but in the process, God destroys everything they hold dear (like a moth consumes everything, v. 11). The psalmist understands the need for punishment, but what God is doing to his life is too much and going too far for a life that lasts only a moment.

The poet never specifies what it is that he believes God is doing. Most interpreters guess that the trouble involves some illness or injury (based on the terms in vv. 10–11). In any event, the proposed solution is unexpected. The poet asks God to consider him as an "alien" or a "sojourner like all my ancestors" (v. 12).

In view of the brevity of life (vv. 4–5) the idea that humans are just sojourners passing through life is apt. But this is no innocent request. For God to accept the poet's status as an alien or sojourner has ethical implications. God has taught Israel to treat sojourners fairly, hosted and accepted, and never harmed (Exod. 22:21; 23:9). So for the poet, if humans are God's sojourners, the implication is that God must stop mistreating them and taking away "their desires" or "what is dear to them" (NRSV). Not even Israel is allowed to treat aliens like that.

If God is not willing to accept and treat the poet as a sojourner, then the poet reaches for a final alternative: please, just leave me alone so that I may smile again (v. 13). A little joy, a little relief for a short life does not seem like too much to ask.

The psalmist did not want to speak, and now we understand why. But before we dismiss his poem as the ranting of one who has lost faith, consider the deep faith exhibited in the psalm. The poet's only hope is God; he has nowhere else to turn (v. 7). He postpones his speech out of concern for unbelievers or the wicked who will not understand. Because the psalmist believes in the sovereignty of God he speaks these words and addresses them to God. If he did not believe or have relationship with God, he would not speak at all.

For Those Who Sing Psalm 39

This is a psalm that the poet may have never intended to write. He knew that if he began to speak, his words would indict God, but faith and genuine relationship do not let us off so easily. We, like the poet, must speak the truth of our lives, the whole truth, and nothing but the truth, even if it questions God. Before we dismiss this poem as faithless, listen for the deep convictions exhibited in the psalm. Yes, the poet charges God—life is short, difficult, and many long for just a little reprieve, just a little joy in life. But God remains sovereign, the poet's and our only hope.

Glenn Pemberton

Lord God, Please Hear My Prayer

Psalm 39

Norman Horn | Katelyn Horn

Lord God, Please Hear My Prayer

Let Me Know My Sinful Failings

Psalm 39

Mark Shipp

Konstantin Zhigulin

Let Me Know My Sinful Failings

Psalm 40

Translation

For the director. A song of David.

*1 I waited and waited for the LORD and he turned to me; he heard my cry for help.
†2 He lifted me up from a desolate pit, from deep, deep mud; he set my feet on a rock, steadying my steps.
†3 He put a new song in my mouth, a song of praise to our God; many saw and were amazed and put their trust in the LORD.

*4 Blessed are those who have made the LORD their trust and do not turn to the proud or those entangled in lies.

†5 Many, O LORD my God, are the wonderful deeds that you have done and your attention to us; no one compares to you. Were I to report and tell, they are beyond counting.

†6 You do not desire sacrifices and gifts. You have opened my ears.[a] You do not ask for whole offerings or sin offerings.
*7 Then I said, "Here I am! It is written about me in the scroll of the book.
*8 I desire to do your will, my God; your teaching is within me."

†9 I have told about the good news of victory in the great assembly; I have not restrained my lips, O LORD; you know this.
†10 I did not hide your victory in my heart; I have spoken about your faithfulness and your salvation. I have not hidden your steadfast love or your truth from the great assembly.

*11 Come, LORD, do not withhold your compassion from me; may your steadfast love and your truth always keep me.

†12 Troubles have gathered about me beyond number; my iniquities have overwhelmed me so that I am unable to see. They outnumber the hairs of my head so that I have lost heart.

†13 Be pleased, LORD, to deliver me! LORD, hurry to help me!

†14 May those who seek to end my life be shamed and disgraced together. May those who want to hurt me be turned back and shamed.[b]
†15 May those who say to me, "Aha! Aha!" be appalled because of their shame.

*16 But may all those who seek you exult and rejoice in you. May those who love your salvation say continually, "Great is the LORD."

*[17] I am afflicted and needy; may the LORD consider me. You are my help and rescue, my God; do not delay.

[a] Literally, "ears you have dug for me." See explanation below.

[b] Against more literal translations that maintain the Hebrew Verb/Subject order (e.g., NRSV, NASV), I have placed the participial phrases before the verbs in verses 14–15 (as in common English usage; so also TNIV, NJPS) rather than after the verb (as in common Hebrew).

Structure and Poetry

The two halves of the psalm are so distinct that at first glance, it appears that two psalms may have been inadvertently combined in one chapter (vv. 1–10 and vv. 11–17; cf. Ps. 27). In fact, verses 13–17 are nearly identical with Psalm 70. Which came first, however, 40:13–17 or 70:1–5, is difficult to discern. In any case, on a closer reading of Psalm 40, the repetition of vocabulary and coherency of theme bring the two halves together as one united psalm.

Theology and Application

In the first part, the psalmist recounts an earlier time when the LORD delivered him from deadly trouble (vv. 1–3). In response to this dramatic rescue, the psalmist sings a "new song" scripted by God's action: those who trust the LORD are blessed (v. 4), God has great concern for his people (v. 5), and the LORD desires obedience over mere sacrifice (vv. 6–8). Most of all, the psalmist emphasizes that he gladly told others about the LORD's work in his life; he has not stayed silent or hidden the good news (vv. 9–10).

Within this part of the psalm, verses 6–8 pose special difficulties. The phrase "you have opened my ears" comes from a more literal phrase "you have dug ears for me" (v. 6). God has enabled the poet to have a deeper or better understanding, specifically a greater insight into sacrifice. Sacrifice accompanied by a psalm was a customary way to express thanksgiving for the LORD's deliverance. What the psalmist now realizes is that God's desire has more to do with the person than the gift. Through dialectic negation that exaggerates the negative in order to give emphasis to the positive, the poet proclaims a negative overstatement (God does not desire sacrifice or gifts) in order to emphasize a positive idea (God desires the person and his or her obedience). And so the psalmist presents himself ("Here I am") to the LORD (vv. 7–8). Similar ideas are expressed elsewhere in the Old Testament (Hosea 6:6; Isa. 1:12–17). The phrase "The scroll of the book" is ambiguous. It may refer to a scroll in which the psalmist has written about God's help and that the psalmist now presents in the temple. Or if we take the psalmist to be the king, the scroll may refer to Deuteronomy 17:17–19. Hebrews 10:5 adapts verses 6–8 from the Septuagint in order to describe Jesus' self-sacrificial work.

In the second half of the psalm, the psalmist is once again in a troubled situation (v. 12) and needs the LORD to intervene and to do so quickly (vv. 11, 13, 17). One part of the problem is his own failure (v. 12). The primary issue is other people who are trying to hurt or even destroy the psalmist, perhaps even because of the psalmist's determination to credit the LORD with his prior rescue (vv. 14–15). The poet's request in verse 16 unites the two halves of the psalm; just as the psalmist rejoiced in the LORD's deliverance and told the good news to others (vv. 9–10), he asks that all those who seek the LORD's help—as he does again in verses 11–17—may rejoice and speak about the LORD's greatness. His prayer for himself and others is to have the opportunity to tell the good news of God's victory. Such retelling of what God has done is a key component of thanksgiving. Like the psalmist, we should gratefully recount to others what God has done in our lives.

For Those Who Sing Psalm 40

What is your story, your "new song" about God's work in your life? "As for me," the poet of Psalm 40 claims, "I could never keep a secret or tell a lie. I've told everyone—openly, vibrantly, about God's wonderful work. After all, if not for God, I never would have survived. I must remember, because I cannot lie. Once again I am so overwhelmed by troubles that I cannot see a way forward. Life is like that—up and down, back and forth." So what is your story? What memory of God will sustain you when the bottom drops out of life again? "We remember, O LORD. Please help, please hurry."

Glenn Pemberton

How Many Are Your Wonders, Lord?

Psalm 40

Mark Shipp & Jerry Shipp

Randy Daw

How Many Are Your Wonders, Lord?

I Waited Patiently for God

(congregational version)

Linda Gregersen | *Psalm 40:1–5* | Matt Roberson

Choral

I Waited Patiently for God

(choral version)

Psalm 40:1–5

Linda Gregersen

Matt Roberson

Sing Great Is the Lord!

Psalm 40

Jerry Shipp Katelyn Horn

praise and lift to their God a vic - to - ri - ous shout. Sing
they sing praise,
"Great is the Lord" all their days, sing "Great is the Lord" all their
"Great is the Lord,"
days, sing "Great is the Lord," they sing
"Great is the Lord,"
"Great is the Lord," sing "Great is the Lord" all their days.
all their days.

Psalm 41

Translation

For the director: A song of David.

1 Blessed is the person who considers the poor; when he is in trouble the LORD will deliver him.
2 The LORD protects him and gives him life; he is blessed in the land. You do not hand him over to the desires of his enemy.
3 The LORD sustains him on his sickbed; you change every place he lies down when he is ill.

4 I myself said, "O LORD, have mercy on me! Heal me! I have sinned against you."
5 My enemies say terrible things about me: "When will he die and his name be wiped out?"
6 When he comes to see me he imagines the worst; he collects malicious lies and then goes out to tell everyone.
7 Everyone who hates me gossips about me; they invent terrible things about me:
8 "A devilish disease has been put on him! He will never get up from where he has lain down!"
9 Even my friend whom I trusted, who ate with me, is kicking me *while I am down*.[a]
10 But you, O LORD, have mercy on me and lift me up; let me repay them!
11 By this I know that you are pleased with me, that my enemy does not shout victory over me.
12 And as for me, you uphold me in my integrity and set me in your presence forever.

13 Blessed be the LORD God of Israel from everlasting to everlasting. Amen. Amen.

[a] Literally, "he makes great against me [his] heel."

Structure and Poetry

Psalm 41 opens by pronouncing a blessing on those who care for those in need (vv. 1–3). The poet then recounts his own crisis, perhaps a serious illness, in which he appealed to the LORD while others not only failed to help, but took advantage of his weakness (vv. 4–10). Looking back on this event, the poet concludes that the LORD did intervene on his behalf and against his enemies (vv. 11–12), affirming the earlier promise that the LORD will sustain those who care for others (vv. 1–3).

The doxology in verse 13 is not part of the psalm but denotes the end of Book I of the Psalms. The editors placed this and other doxologies at the conclusion of each of the five books (Pss. 72:18–19; 89:52; 106:48; and Ps. 150).

Theology and Application

As in Psalm 40, a crucial element of thanksgiving is a report about what God has done that merits thanksgiving. Here in Psalm 41, the psalmist recites his prior lament, to which the LORD responded (vv. 4–10), in order to give thanks and encourage those "who consider the poor" (those who are "weak" [NIV], "helpless" [NASV], or physically ill).

The poet begins by speaking a blessing over all who take an active concern for those who are sick, perhaps a blessing for those who looked after him when he was ill (v. 1). For these caretakers, he prays that the LORD will deliver them when they face trouble (v. 1), keeping them alive (v. 2), and sustaining them on their sickbed (v. 3). In addition, he asks that while they are ill, the LORD not hand them over to enemies who would take advantage of their weakness (v. 2).

Originally, the lament in verses 4–10 must have sounded like the last words of a dying man. He was seriously ill, by his reckoning, as the result of some unspecified sin for which he asks forgiveness (v. 4). The connection of sin and disease was a common idea in ancient Israel, an equation that the book of Job and Jesus warn must be applied with caution. Just because a person is sick does not mean that he or she has sinned (Luke 13:1–5). The psalmist's second request regards people who hope that the poet will die and cease to exist in any form—reputation, children, memory ("his name be wiped out," v. 5). They are two-faced. When they come to visit him they say all the acceptable things (e.g., "we hope you get well soon"). But they are bogus. Their visits are nothing more than reconnaissance missions to get more grist for the rumor mill (v. 6). They assume that the psalmist must have committed some terrible sin; so they visit only to gather clues and then go out to tell everyone what they have seen. Despite their words, they do not believe or want the psalmist to recover (vv. 6–8). Their smear campaign hurts, but the poet is too weak and sick to respond. Much worse, his trusted friend has also betrayed him (v. 9).

Helpless to defend himself, the psalmist asks God to intervene (v. 10). His request, "let me repay them," is unusual. Normally, a psalmist will ask God to repay his enemies. Here, however, the idea may still be that God's action of raising him up (i.e., healing him) will be the repayment the poet gives the enemies. When God heals him, it will prove the enemies were wrong and cause them shame.

The psalmist recovered from his brush with death and so has confidence in God and his relationship with him (vv. 11–12) and encouragement for other believers who find themselves in distress (vv. 1–3). It would be a misreading of the poetry, however, to assert from verses 1–3 that God sustains and heals every follower who makes an appeal. Psalms do not function as wholesale legal guarantees. Here, the writer asserts confidence in the LORD's support because of his healing (v. 11). But like the equation of "sin leads to suffering," the reason for blessing or its absence should also be discerned with caution.

In addition to appropriate caution regarding simplistic and inadequate formulas connecting sin and disease, or a believer's appeal and God's healing, Psalm 41 also reminds us of core life principles: it is the person who expresses concern for the poor that catches the Lord's attention and blessing, while an enemy is one who thinks and speaks the worst about others. While we may all want God's favor or healing, the more important issue is who we are—the friend to those in need or their enemy?

For Those Who Sing Psalm 41

May God bless the nurses, the doctors, the orderlies, the friends who sit at our bedside through the night, the people who clean our homes and sustain us with food when we are ill. The poet of Psalm 41 was critically ill; everyone thought he would die. So some took advantage of him and some friends abandoned him, but not God, and not those special people who care about the sick and poor in health. So today may God bless you:

> May God tend to your pain and weakness as you have tended to us.
> May God be compassionate to you, as you have had compassion on us.
> May God heal you, as you have been a conduit of God's healing to us.

Glenn Pemberton

Regard Me, Everlasting God

Psalm 41

Sarah Shipp | Randy Daw

Lord, Have Mercy

Psalm 41

Chris Stivers

Chris Stivers

Lord, Have Mercy

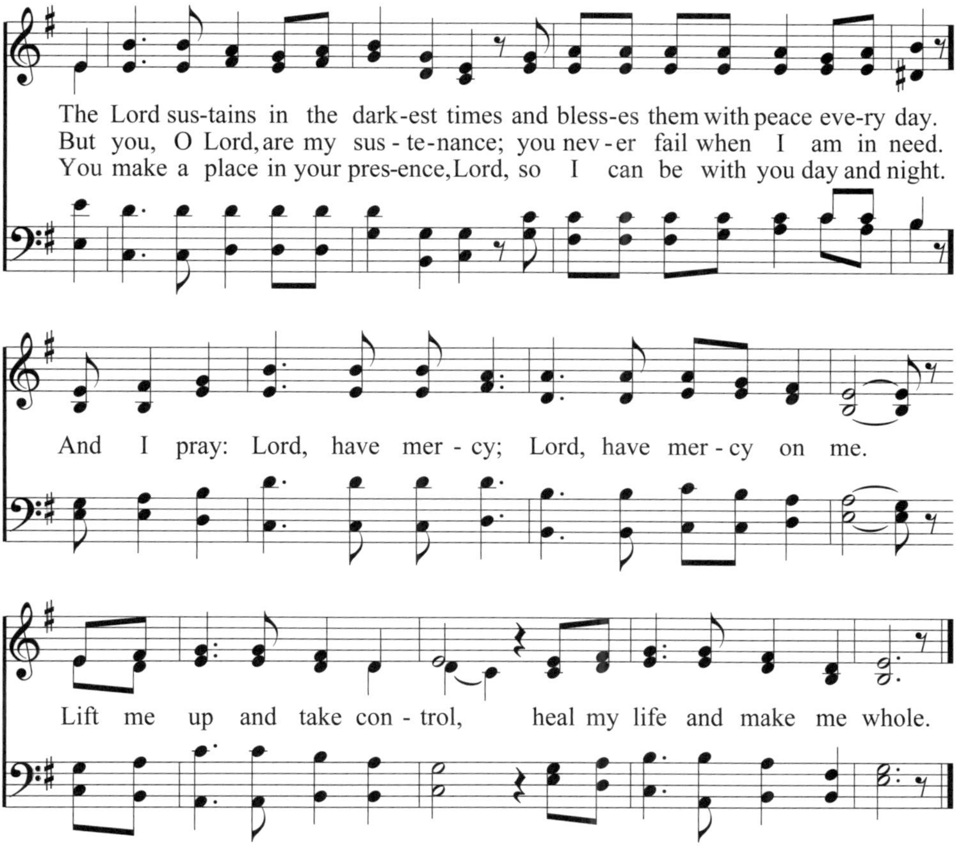

Select Bibliography on the Book of Psalms, Metrical Psalters, and Hymnals

Commentaries and Monographs

Allen, Leslie C. *Psalms 101–150*. Word Biblical Commentary 21. Waco: Word Books, 1983.

Anderson, Bernard W. *Out of the Depths: The Psalms Speak for Us Today*. 3rd, revised and expanded edition. Philadelphia: Westminster, 2000.

Ash, Anthony L. and Clyde M. Miller. *Psalms*. Living Word Commentary. Austin: Sweet, 1980.

Bellinger, W. H. *Psalms: Reading and Studying the Book of Praises*. Peabody, MA: Hendrickson, 1990.

Braun, Joachim. *Music in Ancient Israel/Palestine: Archaeological, Written, and Comparative Sources*. Translated by Douglas Stott. Grand Rapids: Eerdmans, 2002.

Brueggemann, Walter. *The Message of the Psalms: A Theological Commentary*. Minneapolis: Augsburg, 1984.

______. *The Psalms and the Life of Faith*. Patrick D. Miller, ed. Minneapolis: Fortress, 1995.

Broyles, Craig C. *Psalms*. New International Biblical Commentary. Peabody, MA: Hendrickson, 1999.

de Claisse-Walford, Nancy L. *Introduction to the Psalms. A Song from Ancient Israel*. St. Louis: Chalice, 2004.

Craigie, Peter C. *Psalms 1–50*. Word Biblical Commentary 19. Waco: Word Books, 1983.

Crenshaw, James L. *The Psalms: An Introduction*. Grand Rapids: Eerdmans, 2001.

Davidson, Robert. *The Vitality of Worship: A Commentary on the Book of Psalms*. Grand Rapids: Eerdmans, 1998.

Eaton, John. *The Psalms: A Historical and Spiritual Commentary with an Introduction and New Translation*. London: Continuum, 2005.

Goldingay, John. *Psalms, Vol. 1: Psalms 1–41*. Baker Commentary on the Old Testament. Grand Rapids: Baker Academic, 2006.

______. *Psalms, Vol. 2: Psalms 42–89*. Baker Commentary on the Old Testament. Grand Rapids: Baker Academic, 2007.

______. *Psalms, Vol. 3: Psalms 90–150*. Baker Commentary on the Old Testament. Grand Rapids: Baker Academic, 2008.

Green, Fred Pratt. 1972. © 1989 Hope Publishing Co., Carol Stream, Ill. 60188.

Gruber, Mayer I., ed. *Rashi's Commentary on Psalms*. Philadelphia: Jewish Publication Society, 2007.

Holladay, William L. *The Psalms Through Three Thousand Years: Prayerbook of a Cloud of Witnesses*. Minneapolis: Fortress, 1993.

Lewis, C. S. *Reflections on the Psalms*. New York: Harcourt Brace Jovanovich, 1958.

Limburg, James. *Psalms*. Westminster Bible Companion. Louisville: Westminster/John Knox, 2000.

Mays, James L. *The Lord Reigns: A Theological Handbook to the Psalms*. Louisville: Westminster/John Knox, 2004.

______. *Psalms*. Interpretation Commentary. Louisville: John Knox, 1994.

McCann, J. Clinton, Jr. "The Book of Psalms: Introduction, Commentary, and Reflections." Pages 639–1280 in The New Interpreter's Bible, vol. IV. Edited by Leander Keck, et. al. Nashville: Abingdon, 1996.

______. *A Theological Introduction to the Book of Psalms: The Psalms as Torah*. Nashville: Abingdon, 1993.

Miller, Patrick D. *Interpreting the Psalms* (Philadelphia: Fortress, 1986).

______. *They Cried to the Lord: The Form and Theology of Biblical Prayer*. Minneapolis: Fortress, 1994.
Pollard, Adelaide A. "Have Thine Own Way, Lord," originally published in the *Northfield Hymnal with Alexander's Supplement*, 1907.
Selderhuis, Herman J. *Calvin's Theology of the Psalms*. Grand Rapids: Baker Academic, 2007.
Simon, Uriel. *Four Approaches to the Book of Psalms: From Saadiah Gaon to Abraham ibn Ezra*. Albany, NY: SUNY Press, 1991).
Tanner, Beth LaNeel. *The Psalms for Today*. Louisville: Westminster/John Knox, 2008.
Tate, Marvin E. *Psalms 51–100*. Word Biblical Commentary 20. Waco: Word Books, 1990.
Waltke, Bruce and James Houston. *The Psalms as Christian Worship: A Historical Commentary*. Grand Rapids: Eerdmans, 2010.
Warton, Thomas. *The History of English Poetry: from the Eleventh to the Seventeenth Century.* New York: G. P Putnam & Sons, 1870.
Wilson, Gerald H. *Psalms Volume 1*. The NIV Application Commentary. Grand Rapids: Zondervan, 2002.
Witvliet, John D. *The Biblical Psalms in Christian Worship*. Grand Rapids: Eerdmans, 2007.

Metrical Psalters, or Hymnals Containing Psalm Sections

Ainsworth, Henry. *The Ainsworth Psalter*. Amsterdam: 1612.
The Board of Education and Publication, Reformed Presbyterian Church of North America. *The Book of Psalms for Singing*. Pittsburgh: Crown & Covenant, 1998.
Christ Church. *Cantus Christi*. Moscow, Idaho: Canon Press, 2002.
Christian Reformed Church in North America. *Psalter Hymnal*. Grand Rapids: CRC, 1988.
The Church of England. *Hymns Ancient and Modern: New Standard Edition*. Norwich: Canterbury, 1983.
The Commission on Worship of the Lutheran Church—Missouri Synod. *Lutheran Service Book*. St. Louis: Concordia, 2006.
Johnson, Clarence R. *Psalms to Sing*. Elizabethtown: Exhorter Publications International, 1995.
Livingston, Neil. *The Scottish Metrical Psalter of 1835*. Glasgow: Maclure & Macdonald, 1864.
Mather, Richard, John Eliot, et. al. *The Whole Booke of Psalmes, Faithfully Translated into English Metre* ("*The Bay Psalm Book*"). Cambridge, MA: Stephen Daye, 1640.
Morgan, Michael. *Psalter for Christian Worship*. Louisville: Witherspoon Press and the Office of Theology and Worship, Presbyterian Church (U.S.A.) and Atlanta: Columbia Theological Seminary, 1999.
Presbyterian Church of America, Reformed Presbyterian Church of North America. *Trinity Psalter*. Pittsburgh: Crown & Covenant, 2000.
The Standing Committee for the Publication of the Book of Praise. *The Book of Praise of the Canadian Reformed Church: Anglo-Genevan Psalter*. Winnipeg, MN: Canadian Reformed Church, 1984.
Sternhold, Thomas, John Hopkins, et. al. *The Whole Book of Psalms, Collected into English Metre*. Oxford: Clarendon, 1812.
Tel, Martin, Joyce Borger, and John D. Witvliet. *Psalms for All Seasons: A Complete Psalter for Worship*. Grand Rapids: Brazos, 2012.

Other Hymnals

Fettke, Tom, ed. *The Hymnal for Worship and Celebration*. Waco: Word Music, 1986.
Howard, Alton, ed. *Songs of Faith and Praise*. West Monroe, LA: Howard, 1984.
Jorgenson, E. L., ed. *Great Songs of the Church, Number Two*. Hammond, IN: Great Songs, 1975.
McCann, Forrest M., ed. *Great Songs of the Church*. Revised Edition. Abilene, TX: ACU Press, 1986.
Sims, Walter Hines, ed. *The Baptist Hymnal*. Nashville: Convention Press, 1956.
The Standing Commission on Church Music. *The Hymnal* (1982). New York: CPI, 1985.

Index of Contributors by Composition or Commentary

* = arrangement only
italic = psalm commentaries

Index of Song Titles

Metrical Index

SM = Short Meter (6.6.8.6)
CM = Common Meter (8.6.8.6)
LM = Long Meter (8.8.8.8)
D = doubled

Index of Chants and Unison Melodies

Index of Adapted Tunes

Index of Song Difficulty

Psalm 27 (Strength of My Life)
Psalm 28 (In Your Refuge)
Psalm 29 (Ascribe to the Lord)
Psalm 31 (My Life Is Filled with Deep Distress)
Psalm 33 (Sing Praise!)
Psalm 34 (Taste and See that the Lord Is Good)
Psalm 35 (Contend, O Lord, Contend)
Psalm 37 (Trust Your Ways unto Jehovah)
Psalm 41 (Regard Me, Everlasting God)

Psalm 3 (Strong Defender)
Psalm 4 (Answer Me When I Call)
Psalm 6 (Return, O Lord)
Psalm 6 (Lamentation in the Night)
Psalm 13 (How Long?)
Psalm 14 (The Fool Has Said, "There Is No God")
Psalm 19 (More Precious than Gold)
Psalm 24:3–5 (Who Shall Ascend?)
Psalm 25 (Turn to Me, O Holy Lord)
Psalm 34 (I Bless the Lord Both Day and Night)
Psalm 35 (Contend, O Lord)
Psalm 38 (Do Not Abandon Me)
Psalm 38 (Still I Wait, O Lord)
Psalm 39 (Lord God, Please Hear My Prayer)
Psalm 39 (Let Me Know My Sinful Failings)
Psalm 40 (Sing Great Is the Lord!)
Psalm 40:1–5 (I Waited Patiently for God [congregational version])
Psalm 41 (Lord, Have Mercy)

Psalm 1 (How Blest Is the Man)
Psalm 1 (Blessed Is the Man Who Trusts in God)
Psalm 18:21–31 (I Have Kept the Ways of Jehovah)
Psalm 20 (In the Day of Distress)
Psalm 20 (He Will Answer)
Psalm 25 (Preserve My Soul)
Psalm 33 (His Steadfast Love Fills All the Earth)
Psalm 40:1–5 (I Waited Patiently for God [choral version])

Contributors to Timeless and Timeless Committee Members

Cynthia Agnell,* *Austin, Texas.* Cynthia is the editor of the newsletter and chairperson of the Associates at Austin Graduate School of Theology.

Craig Bowman,◊ *Rochester, Michigan.* Dr. Bowman is professor of Old Testament at Rochester College and has co-directed numerous archaeological digs at En Hazeva, Israel (biblical Tamar).

Jack Boyd, ‡ *Abilene, Texas.* Dr. Boyd, a retired professor of music at Abilene Christian University, was music editor for the hymnal *Great Songs of the Church, Revised.*

Michele Broadway,* *Austin, Texas.* Michele holds the bachelor's of music education from Abilene Christian University. She has taught band and secondary math and science in Texas public schools and now teaches mathematics at Brentwood Christian School in Austin, Texas.

D. J. Bulls,* *Arlington, Texas.* In addition to his work as minister of music and worship at North Davis Church of Christ, D. J. arranges music and is pursuing a doctorate in choral music.

Brad Everett Cawyer, ‡ Saint Petersburg, Russia. Brad, a composer of hymns in Russian and English, has a master of music in orchestral and operatic conducting from Rimsky-Korsakov Conservatory and sings with the musical ensemble *Psalom.*

Laura Kate Collum, ‡ *South Orange, New Jersey.* Kate is a Texas native who studied piano and voice as a child and is now an attorney in New York City.

M. L. Daniels,* ‡ *Austin, Texas.* Dr. Daniels, retired ACU music professor, has won numerous composition contests and published more than one hundred musical works.

Jeremy Daw, ‡ *Oakland, California.* Soon to be an attorney, Jeremy plays guitar, bass, and trumpet and writes religious and secular songs.

Randy Daw,* ‡ *Greenville, Texas.* Randy has a degree in music education from West Texas State University; he is a minister as well as the composer and arranger of many *a cappella* spiritual songs.

J. Andrew Dearman,◊ *Houston, Texas.* Dr. Dearman is professor of Old Testament and director of Fuller Theological Seminary, Texas.

Debbie Dorman,* ‡ *Austin, Texas.* Debbie is the director of worship ministries at Hope Chapel in Austin, Texas, and the composer of many published hymns.

Jack Dorman,* *Austin, Texas.* Jack is the retired senior pastor of Hope Chapel in Austin, Texas.

Ashley Gay, ‡ *Boston, Massachusetts.* Ashley has a master of arts in theological studies from Austin Graduate School of Theology and a Master of Arts in Theological Research (theology and the arts) from Andover Newton Theological School.

Michael R. Greene, ‡ *Winchester, Indiana.* With a master of music in choral conducting, Michael directs the choir at Winchester Community High School in Indiana and serves as the music editor of *Praise for the Lord* hymnal.

Linda McClurg Gregersen, ‡ *Mt. Vernon, Missouri.* Linda, a former missionary to Zambia, has directed a children's chorus for many years and enjoys meditating on the psalms and writing metrical psalms.

†**Jennifer Hall,** ‡ *San Marcos, Texas.* Jennifer was a student at Austin Graduate School of Theology until her death at age 26 in June, 2000. She is survived by her daughter Madison and husband Todd.

Mark W. Hamilton,◊ *Abilene, Texas.* Dr. Hamilton teaches Old Testament at Abilene Christian University, where he is also associate dean of the Graduate School of Theology. He holds a Ph.D. in Old Testament from Harvard University.

Katelyn Horn,* ‡ *Columbus, Ohio.* Katelyn Horn holds a B.M. in piano performance and an M.M. in music theory from the University of Texas, Austin. She is currently a Ph.D. fellow in music theory and cognition at Ohio State University in Columbus, Ohio.

Norman Horn,* ‡ *Austin, Texas.* Norman has been a worship minister at the University Avenue Church of Christ while earning an M.S. and Ph.D. in chemical engineering from the University of Texas at Austin, along with an M.A. in theological studies from Austin Graduate School of Theology.

Marva L. Hughes,* ‡ *Weatherford, Texas.* Marva is a graduate of Abilene Christian University, a licensed medical technologist, and composer of hymns.

Heath Jones, *Edmond, Oklahoma.* ‡ Dr. Jones is associate professor of music at Oklahoma Christian University and a professional performer in the Oklahoma City area.

Kathleen Kirkland-Kanewske, ‡ *Austin, Texas.* Kathleen is head of school and music director of Regina Mater, a homeschool initiative of Catholic families, as well as producer of the CD "Heavenwards, Always—The Childlike Spirit of Father Joseph Kentenich in Dachau."

Felix E. Kneuper, ‡ *Fort Stockton, Texas.* Currently serving as pulpit minister for the Fort Stockton, Texas, Church of Christ, Felix's music credits include principal horn player for the Symphony of the Hills, Houston Sinfonietta, Blasmusik Texas, and scoring music for the PBS series "A Writer's Exchange."

Keith Lancaster, ‡ *Tulsa, Oklahoma.* Keith is the president and chief composer for Acappella Ministries, and is currently serving with his wife Sharon as international "musicianaries" for the Park Plaza Church of Christ in Tulsa, Oklahoma.

Jeffrey Taylor Matteson, ‡ *Luling, Texas.* Jeff is evangelist for the Luling Church of Christ and a vocalist, instrumentalist, and composer who frequently performs with the musical ensemble *Psalom*.

Rachel McInturff, ‡ *Austin, Texas.* Dr. McInturff serves as the associate director of the Armstrong Community Music School as well as being a freelance composer, arranger, and recording engineer.

Brad Merrell,* *Austin, Texas.* Brad has performed in or directed several Gilbert and Sullivan operettas and is a past president of The Gilbert and Sullivan Society of

Austin. He is currently in The Sweet Expressions and sings with the chorus at Brentwood Oaks Church of Christ.

Dan Merrell,* *Austin, Texas.* Dan, an artist specializing in watercolors, serves as director of the Brentwood Oaks Church of Christ chorus.

Glenn Pemberton,◊ *Abilene, Texas.* Dr. Pemberton is Associate Professor of Old Testament in the College of Biblical Studies at Abilene Christian University.

Gary Pendergrass, ‡ *Greenville, Texas.* A software engineering manager, for the last twenty years Gary has written songs for and sung in the *a cappella* gospel quartet *Family Reunion*.

Sean Pullen, ‡ *Abilene, Texas.* Dr. Pullen is director of choral activities at Abilene Christian University.

Jack R. Reese,* ‡ *Abilene, Texas.* Trained as a pianist, Dr. Reese is dean of the College of Biblical Studies and Graduate School of Theology at Abilene Christian University. He is also a professor of worship and preaching.

Matt Roberson, ‡ *Montgomery, Alabama.* Dr. Roberson is chairman of the Department of Fine Arts at Faulkner University.

Russell D. Scott, ‡ *Richardson, Texas.* Russell has a music degree from Harding University and is owner of Allegro Music Academy in Dallas.

Gina Shipp, ‡ *Austin, Texas.* Gina is an author and musician.

Glover Shipp, ‡ *Edmond, Oklahoma.* Dr. Shipp is a retired writer, editor, poet, and composer of approximately 150 hymns, many of which have been published.

Jerry Shipp,* ‡ *Austin, Texas.* Jerry, a marriage and family therapist for twenty-seven years, is co-creator of an oratorio based on *Hinds' Feet on High Places*.

R. Mark Shipp,* ‡◊ *Austin, Texas.* Dr. Shipp is the Pat Harrell Professor of Old Testament at Austin Graduate School of Theology. He is co-composer of *Hinds' Feet on High Places* and general editor of *Timeless: Ancient Psalms for the Church Today*.

Rachel Shipp, ‡ *New York City, New York.* Rachel received her B.A. in psychology from Pepperdine University. She is now a graduate student in clinical psychology at Columbia Teacher's College of Columbia University in New York City.

Sarah Shipp, ‡ *Tuscaloosa, Alabama.* Sarah is a graduate student in theatre at the University of Alabama with a B.A. from Harding University, where she minored in English and was a member of the Concert Choir.

Michael E. Showalter, ‡ *Austin, Texas.* Michael performed with the Abilene Christian College Hilltoppers, and he continues to play piano and sing for special events. Currently, he is working part-time as a composer and songwriter, concentrating on church music.

Clyde H. Slimp, ‡ *Mustang, Oklahoma.* Clyde is preaching minister for the Lakehoma Church of Christ and a member of ASCAP and NSAI.

Ruth Ann Somervell,* ‡ *Austin, Texas.* Ruth Ann, a piano teacher and professional composer, holds a Bachelor of Music degree in Choral Music Studies from the University of Texas at Austin.

Becky Stewart,* *Austin, Texas.* Becky is a sixth grade teacher with many years of experience singing in college, community, and church choral groups.

Chris Stivers, ‡ *Agoura Hills, California.* Chris is part of the web and multimedia team at Pepperdine University where he also teaches mediated communication and is musical director for the annual student production *Songfest.*

James Tackett,* ‡ Austin, Texas. James retired from NCR Corp as a computer technician. He teaches at the ACU Singing School and owns The Paperless Hymnal® and Austin Christian Acappella Music.

Kathy A. Thompson, ‡ *Edmond, Oklahoma.* Dr. Thompson is department chair and professor of music at Oklahoma Christian University.

Martha Pounders Walker, ‡ *Leander, Texas.* Martha, a chaplain ministering to both state and county prisoners and staff, is a published poet, having won several awards.

Paul L. Watson,◊ *Durham, North Carolina.* Dr. Watson is a minister and elder at Cole Mill Road Church of Christ in Durham, North Carolina, and holds a Ph.D. in Old Testament from Yale University.

Mary Elisabeth (Libby) Weed,* *Austin, Texas.* Dr. Weed is Vice President and Principal at Brentwood Christian School, where she has also taught music classes and directed a chorus.

John Willis,◊ *Abilene, Texas.* Dr. Willis is Burton Coffman Distinguished Professor of Biblical Studies in the College of Biblical Studies at Abilene Christian University. He is the author of many books on the Old Testament.

Judy Witcher,* *Austin, Texas.* Judy, a soloist in the oratorio *Hinds' Feet on High Places,* sings with the Sweet Expressions, a Christian vocal group.

Mel Witcher,* ‡ *Austin, Texas.* Mel, a former band director, has both a bachelor's and a master's in music education.

Ben Witherington, III, ‡ *Wilmore, Kentucky.* Dr. Witherington is Amos Professor of New Testament for Doctoral Studies at Asbury Theological Seminary; he is passionate about music and poetry and was Kentucky Poet of the Month.

Melinda Worley,* *Austin, Texas.* Melinda has a B.S. in education from Abilene Christian University and an M.A.R. from Yale Divinity School, where she sang with the chapel choir. She has produced musicals and taught high school choir at Brentwood Christian School.

Konstantin Zhigulin,‡ *St Petersburg, Russia.* Konstantin's ministry in the church is in congregational worship development: composing new hymns, leading singing, and teaching worship leadership. He is director of the vocal ensemble *Psalom.*

* = member of a *Timeless* review or editorial committee.
‡ = music or lyric contributor to *Timeless.*
◊ = *Timeless* commentator.